THE
BODYBUILDER'S
NUTRITION
BOOK

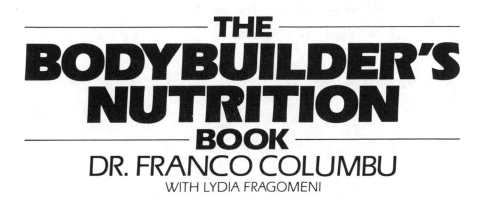

THE
BODYBUILDER'S
NUTRITION
BOOK

DR. FRANCO COLUMBU
WITH LYDIA FRAGOMENI

CONTEMPORARY BOOKS

Library of Congress Cataloging-in-Publication Data

Columbu, Franco.
    The bodybuilder's nutrition book.
    Includes index.
    1. Bodybuilders——Nutrition.   I. Fragomeni, Lydia.
  II. Title.
  TX361.B64C64   1985   613.2   85-13317
  ISBN 0-8092-5457-3

Most of the photographs in this book are by Art Zeller.
Drawings by D. Drake.

Published by Contemporary Books
A division of The McGraw-Hill Companies
4255 West Touhy Avenue, Lincolnwood (Chicago), Illinois 60712-1975 U.S.A.
Copyright © 1985 by Franco Columbu
Printed in the United States of America
International Standard Book Number: 0-8092-5457-3

  04 FGR/FGR 35 34 33 32 31 30 29 28 27 26 25 24 23 22 21 20

CONTENTS

INTRODUCTION

As you probably know, hundreds of books have been written about nutrition, thousands on the subject of dieting. Most of these are geared to the average person and are not concerned with the high level of performance demanded of athletes. Many health-minded individuals want only to look good and feel good; therefore, they rarely focus on the roles played by specific vitamins, minerals, and enzymes or the relative importance of proteins, fats, and carbohydrates. Some are actually surprised to discover that carbohydrates are a source of energy, a fact utilized to full advantage by all championship athletes.

Being a winner in any sport requires rigorous training and the right diet, but these two elements are not the same for all athletes. In most sports the goal is peak performance when playing a game or match. This is based on strength, endurance, and energy, qualities used by bodybuilders mainly in training and not on a field or track. In competitive events one of the prime considerations is muscular size and not athletic ability. Since protein builds muscle tissue, bodybuilders have a high intake compared with other athletes, who need a greater percentage of carbohydrates to perform well during a game.

In addition, if other athletes are highly skilled in their sport, no one cares if they are fat, skinny, or out of proportion. A perfect example of this point is found in the boxing arena. Many fighters have well-defined bodies lacking fat deposits, while others lack definition and look fat; yet both become world champions. On the other hand, bodybuilders must focus on definition and muscularity to sculpture their bodies if they expect a world title.

My recommendations for vitamins and minerals are also directed chiefly at bodybuilders rather than average people or those involved in other sports. Bodybuilders need more vitamin B_6, choline, and calcium than other athletes. Runners may require additional calcium as well as a high intake of vitamin C because they sweat on a continuous basis, but they may not need more choline, used to emulsify fat, or vitamin B_6, which builds muscle.

The information offered in this book is based on research, my personal experience, and direct observation of thousands I have trained. My opinions do not stem from abstract theories founded on computer printouts, but on a vast store of practical experience that has produced remarkable results, leading me and other bodybuilders to the championship levels of our profession and contributing to our good health.

Although the diets are well balanced and meet the nutritional needs of most individuals, they are not ideal for use on a permanent basis. Their purpose is related specifically to competitive bodybuilding, powerlifting, and strength. Throughout the book are my recommendations for learning the needs of your own body. As this awareness grows, make minor changes in the recommended diets to suit your individual preferences. Food tables that appear in Appendix I offer a wide variety of choices to accommodate every taste and are separated into animal and plant categories for the particular benefit of pure vegetarians and ovolactovegetarians. The same attention has been paid to the categorization of vitamins and minerals most directly affecting bodybuilders.

Some people believe they are getting sufficient vitamins and minerals from food sources, but food processing, even in the home, results in loss of nutrients. When following the diets in this book or any other, try gaining a sense of the good or bad effects various foods may have on your body. *If you experience an allergic reaction, identify the specific food causing the problem and eliminate it from your diet.*

Many sections of nutrition books become outdated as time passes because research has become more sophisticated and new theories are constantly proposed. Yet some facts will never change. For example, the quality of protein as listed in the tables in the appendix will remain stable, so you can depend on protein for results. Simplicity is the key to the success of protein in building muscles and gaining definition. Avoid being tempted by current notions to abandon a simple nutritional program in favor of new products like spirulina, liver pills, certain protein powders, and other wonder foods discussed in this book. In my opinion, these products do nothing except delay your progress. Research has shown that most of them are worthless. True, manufacturers run expensive and dynamically designed advertisements describing the high nutritional value of their products, but most of the ingredients are nothing more than fillers. One egg has more protein than an entire can, bottle, or package of these wonder foods. Nothing in this world works magic when it comes to bodybuilding and maintaining buoyant good health. Winning contests, becoming a champion, and keeping in top shape demand many years devoted to training, eating right, and taking supplements in a reasonable measure without going overboard. Equally important is putting an end to time lost by running around in circles looking for magic formulas that come rolling off assembly lines.

Your mental attitude will play an essential role in making things happen. During my last 15 years of training, especially when working out with Arnold Schwarzenegger, we both maintained an unshakable positive attitude every time we went to the gym. For a period of two hours we used our full mental power to such a degree that the weights seemed to dance. We generated so much electricity that it served to stimulate other bodybuilders working out in the same room. Our brutal training periods contributed to getting into top shape fast. After leaving the gym, we ate a great lunch with complete enjoyment, knowing that vitamins and minerals are helpful only when the body is stimulated by hard training and the mind is an instrument made powerful by an aggressive, exciting attitude. In other words, someone having championship potential can eat the best food and take nutritional supplements by the shovel full, yet if he does nothing more than bask in the sunshine, his muscles will not develop—he is not a flower or vegetable that achieves full growth by standing rooted under the sun.

The contents of this book will open your mind to the complex universe existing within your own body and clarify the role nutrition plays in supporting essential life elements. The information that follows is superior to that found in other books on the subject. Although many writers and nutritionists are educationally well-qualified, they lack the practical experience of building their own bodies and evaluating results gained from nutritional programs leading to championship titles.

I have always aimed at utilizing the ultimate level of my potential in bodybuilding and powerlifting, and enjoyed the pleasure of seeing goals accomplished by repeatedly winning titles. Now I am happy to present you with the knowledge gained by this experience, thereby hoping to facilitate your approach to the good health and nutritional habits essential to becoming a champion.

THE
BODYBUILDER'S
NUTRITION
BOOK

ITALY

SARDINIA

1
IN THE BEGINNING

My athletic career began at the age of 14 on the island of Sardinia, where I was born. Although I did some weightlifting, my main interests were soccer and boxing, the most popular Italian sports.

At the small gym where I began training, everyone kept saying, "Athletes must eat better than most people if they want to be outstanding." They believed every good boxer and soccer player should start the day with three or four eggs for breakfast, preferably eaten raw. Also rated high on their list of essential foods were fish and horsemeat. The value of horsemeat was based on the notion that anyone eating it became as strong and enduring as the animal itself. This seemed to make sense, especially when looking at a horse and comparing it to a chicken, goat, or cow.

During those early days in Sardinia, I knew very little about nutrition, so I followed the advice of others training in the gym and ate the types of food they suggested. There was no reason to suppose that specialized diets were needed to become world champion, which was my goal right from the beginning. Little did I realize how much there was to learn, and to keep learning continually, for my dream to become reality.

During my late teenage years, I discovered that my inner needs were not satisfied by either soccer or boxing. Sometimes full involvement in a career or love affair is necessary to realize it's not your thing. True, I was a successful amateur boxer, with a record of 22 knockouts and the Italian lightweight championship, but the opinions of managers and coaches who guided my rate of progress were stifling. Much of their advice was well meant; however, I felt my full potential as an athlete could not be reached training as a boxer.

WEST GERMANY

GERMANY: INTRODUCTION TO BODYBUILDING NUTRITION

In 1966 I began directing my energies to powerlifting, thus becoming my own manager. This proved to be the perfect start for my career in bodybuilding. At the time I was living in Germany and working full-time in a factory while still maintaining the discipline of training regularly. It was at a gym in Munich that I met a young, unknown bodybuilder named Arnold Schwarzenegger. We became training partners and friends almost immediately, trying to beat each other in powerlifting events.

At the gym I also got my first look at some of the top European bodybuilders, including Mr. Italy. Listening to their conversation, I noticed they focused a great deal of attention on nutrition. "Training alone doesn't make you a good bodybuilder," they kept saying. "The right food is just as important for building strong and healthy muscles." Intuitively, I knew they were on the right track, but more than gut feelings caused me to follow their lead. Proof was before my eyes every time one of the top bodybuilders came into the gym and I compared him with others who were training. Not only were their bodies outstanding, but their vitality seemed to stem from some deep source within.

This was another turning point for me. I stopped listening and began questioning Mr. Italy and top German bodybuilders about the type of food they ate. My German was not good at that time, but I found out exactly what I wanted to know: their diets and eating habits were totally different from those of the average person.

For example, most Americans skimp on breakfast during the week, yet on Saturdays and Sundays they stuff themselves with smoked meat, fried potatoes, muffins, French toast, and maple syrup. Lunch usually consists of something appealing sandwiched between two slices of bread, accompanied by a soft drink. Dinner menus are decided by the family cook, a fast food restaurant, or the manufacturer of frozen meals.

The opposite is true of championship bodybuilders, who do not think of food merely as something that tastes good and fills an empty stomach. They see beyond the moment of satisfying hunger to the needs of every cell in the body for nourishment of the organs and tissues that build strong and healthy muscles. To a greater extent than most athletes, competitive bodybuilders are aware that energy is drawn from the entire body; therefore, each meal is planned carefully.

The top bodybuilders I first met in Germany started the day by taking vitamins and minerals, followed by three eggs and some pineapple. I used to wonder about the pineapple because in Sardinia it was considered an exotic fruit. Only later, when studying for my Ph.D. in nutrition, did I learn it contained unique enzymes, aiding the digestion of protein. Pineapple was sometimes also included on the lunch menu, but the dominating food for both lunch and dinner was a large piece of fish or chicken. Many of the bodybuilders were into eating liver and other organ meats, such as heart and kidneys. Horsemeat was also favored. The myth of becoming as strong as a horse by eating its flesh is popular throughout Europe; however, the bodybuilders in Germany also knew it was high in protein with less fat than other red meat.

I became convinced that nutrition was a large part of winning bodybuilding. In those days I knew very little about the metabolism of proteins, fats, and carbohydrates in relation to body chemistry. This would come with learning and experimenting over the years. At the time I felt it wise to begin by following the example of others while still being attentive to the reaction of my own body to different foods and eating habits. It was then that I began a competitive bodybuilder's diet by having four to five small meals a day.

As the days went by, I became increasingly fascinated with the idea that a particular selection of foods could make the difference between remaining an average bodybuilder and becoming a champion. Of course, I already knew the importance of discipline, concentration, and developing the right training program for my body. Progress gained through exercise was more easily measured, being something I could see, feel, and judge for myself almost daily. The advantage of eating the right foods would become evident after a longer range of time, although I quickly became equally sensitive to the benefits of eating specific foods and eliminating others from my diet.

COMPETING: VERONA, BRUSSELS, LONDON

In 1968 I entered my first competition in Verona and won the national title of Mr. Italy. More than 40 others had entered the contest, so I took advantage of having so many bodybuilders conveniently gathered to ask questions about the foods they ate. I did the same thing in Brussels two months later when I won the title of Mr. Europe. A great deal of the information I gathered was similar, but I had the gut feeling that something highly important was still to be learned. An opportunity to find out what it was arose six months later when I entered the Mr. Universe competition in London.

Right from the start, it was obvious that the most outstanding bodybuilders were American. Only they had real depth and clarity of muscle, in addition to the symmetry Europeans mainly trained for in the 1960s. I wondered what made the big difference. After all, lifting weights is the same whether the weights are lifted in Europe or in the United States. We all have the same force of gravity to contend with. The secret of the Americans' superior physique seemed to lie in a specialized diet, enabling them to achieve a *defined look,* today's primary concern of winning bodybuilders.

At the time of the competition in London I spoke no English, but fortunately an Italian friend who did was available.

"Find out what the Americans are eating," I told him.

When my friend returned he shrugged his shoulders and reported, "They all have different diets."

As I began questioning him about specific foods included in
their diets, a similarity I was sure existed immediately became
obvious. Every American bodybuilder, without exception, was
eating food high in protein, very low in fat, and moderate in
carbohydrates. This discovery was the turning point in my search
for the right nutritional program.

Here I would like to stress the fact that the average diet of
people in Western countries is high in fat and carbohydrates but
low in protein. Almost the exact opposite was true of the American
bodybuilders I first met in London. Could this difference be one of
the key factors in attaining that finished look given only by
emphasis on definition?

AMERICA

THE AMERICANS

I continued asking questions, aiming to pinpoint the Americans'
main source of protein, carbohydrates, and fat. I learned that the
intake of protein was provided chiefly by eggs and fish, with a tight
rein held on eating bacon, ham, sausages, and other meats high in
fat content. Carbohydrates came primarily from fresh fruits and
vegetables as they did when I lived at home in Sardinia. A point
was made to avoid potato chips, French fries, and all crunchy

snacks wrapped in cellophane paper or plastic bags. Even more to be avoided as evil demons were sugar-loaded foods such as candy and pastry. Instead of having a piece of pie, cake, or ice cream for dessert like their fellow Americans, the bodybuilders ate fruit, having grapes, an apple, or a pear, particularly before training at the gym.

PLANNING

Since my interest in bodybuilding had become the focal point of my life, I decided that a specific course of action was essential to becoming Mr. Universe, Mr. Olympia, or a champion of any kind. Believing that the basic principle of making it to the top was divided equally between exercise and nutrition, I planned on putting 50 percent of my efforts into developing the best possible training program for my body and 50 percent into finding the most beneficial diet for muscular growth. In each case I would experiment until maximum results were achieved in a minimum amount of time and with the least effort.

Feeling confident in this direction, I continued my investigation of bodybuilding diets, constantly adding to a store of information on nutrition. When I entered chiropractic college, the courses on nutrition opened my eyes to the relationship between food intake and body chemistry. Each day I discovered fascinating details of my body's makeup that would give me control over its muscular development. Although I learned a great deal, it always seemed there was even more to learn. It is said that "you really have to know something to find out what you don't know." This was certainly true in my case. Often, feeling I finally knew it all, I discovered a new fact that showed I was still making mistakes.

THE LEARNING PROCESS: EXPOSING THE YOGURT MYTH

One of my mistakes involved yogurt. Its value is emphasized by almost every American and European nutritionist. Listed among its beneficial qualities are the high percentage of protein found in every cupful and its ability to activate favorable bacteria in the intestinal tract so other food is easier to digest.

At first yogurt seemed like an ideal food. I wanted the advan-

Note the lack of cuts due to allergic reaction to milk.

tage of high protein in my diet, and equally important was the assurance of having the proper nutrients absorbed by my body through the digestive system. So, I followed the advice of nutritionists, always including one or two cups of yogurt in my daily food intake.

Only after 10 years of learning about nutrition did I discover it has serious disadvantages, especially for competitive bodybuilders. Since the value of yogurt is approved in my earlier books with chapters on nutrition, I would like to discuss several reasons for my change in attitude.

It is true, of course, that yogurt stimulates the formation of intestinal flora, most particularly in the colon, to aid the digestive process. Keeping this in mind, many people have it every day either with meals or for a snack, feeling they have done their part in assuring proper digestion. The value of eating so much yogurt, however, has yet to be proved. Research has shown that only a teaspoon a week is actually necessary to maintain the intestinal flora.

Another point for consideration is the allergic reaction many adults have to dairy products such as cheese, milk, sour cream, ice cream, and yogurt. Adults lack the quantity of rennin found in the digestive systems of babies and small children, enabling most babies and children to eat dairy products without any problems. Yet many babies are cured of colic after pediatricians switch them from milk-based formulas to others made from soybeans.

For bodybuilders, a diet high in yogurt can sabotage the best training program in the world. Yogurt, like most dairy products, causes a layer of fat to form beneath the skin and results in a loss of definition. I came to realize this only after many years of competition. To reach my goal of pure muscularity without a trace of fat, it was necessary to give up yogurt. Therefore, I strongly recommend eliminating it, along with other dairy products, from bodybuilding diets for one or two months before competitive events.

PRACTICAL EXPERIENCE: EXPERIMENTS WITH PROTEIN

Although one of the requirements for my chiropractic degree was 500 class hours of nutrition, and twice this number were needed for my Ph.D., I also learned from practical experience.

Arnold and his *Conan* director, John Milius, visit Franco backstage at the 1981 Mr. Olympia contest.

Knowledge from books makes us aware of possibilities we never knew existed, but this is only part of learning. Some people never go beyond the facts and ideas read in books, thereby missing the most important learning experience of all: discovering for oneself through trial and error.

Arnold and I, for example, experimented a great deal with different diets. It was easy to compare notes constantly because we were training partners. Also, for a time we lived in the same apartment and ate many meals together.

At one point we decided to conduct an experiment to resolve whether meat or fish was the better food to eat, particularly before competitions when we wanted to be in top form. We followed our own training programs but ate fish for one month and switched to meat the following month. The result of this research by the team of Columbu-Schwarzenegger showed that meat provided more energy on a short-term basis, while fish gave us steady energy over a long period of time. In addition, meat had the disadvantage of causing us to gain a greater percentage of fat than muscle.

One of the most damaging practices among bodybuilders is going on a strict diet of meat and water before a major contest and keeping carbohydrate intake at a low level. This is commonly known as a high-protein diet, *but this is not correct*. If you look at the protein tables found in this book, you will see that most meat is high in fat content. This type of diet, therefore, is wrong for bodybuilders. The ideal bodybuilding diet is high in protein, low in fat, and contains enough carbohydrates to maintain the sufficient level of energy needed for hard training.

I've given a few examples of what it's like to learn for yourself. Many others will be found throughout the book. Some may seem simple, but you should realize that sensitivity to your body's responses to diets and training is not acquired overnight, but with time and patience.

SOUND ADVICE: HIGH-QUALITY PROTEIN

Of course, the advice given by experienced bodybuilders was invaluable. I especially recall talking to Reg Park at the start of my career when I knew very little about nutrition. There was a quality about Reg that made me feel he was an honest man, sure to steer me in the right direction.

"What did you eat," I asked him, "to get so muscular and become a champion?"

"Very high-quality protein," he replied, giving an answer I hadn't heard before.

"What is high-quality protein?" I was anxious to know.

"Eggs and fish."

"What about meat?"

"It's good," Reg answered, nodding his head, "but not as good as fish."

Many years of learning have filled my life since I had this conversation with Reg. After much reading, learning, and experimenting, I found nothing that disagreed with his advice. It formed the basis for my own school of thought concerning the best nutritional programs for bodybuilders, although it took a while to discover the exact meaning of *high-quality protein*. This is explained in more detail in Chapter 3.

2
THE BODY AS A UNIVERSE

Most people believe the greatest wonders of the universe are found in outer space, millions of light-years beyond our reach. They are fascinated to learn our galaxy has 100 billion stars and that 10 billion galaxies with about the same number of stars lie within range of our telescopes. Drawing from this knowledge and other scientific data, writers have created some of the most popular movies and television programs shown in America, such as "Star Trek," *Star Wars,* and *E.T.*

Focus on outer space has never been greater than today, yet history shows that men have always had their eyes fixed on the stars. Whether contemplating gods, Martians, or the crew of the Starship *Enterprise* living and loving in outer space, men have always been intrigued by the idea that some kind of life exists in outer space. Here the key word is *life,* defined as the power to grow, reproduce, and regulate activities, using energy from a source such as food or sunlight. To date we have no proof that this power exists anywhere but on earth. It is found in every plant, every form of animal and marine life, and every human being. The power of life in its most marvelous form exists in almost every cell of the 100 trillion that make up our body, a universe we can control to a great extent when its needs and functions are understood.

THE AMOEBA

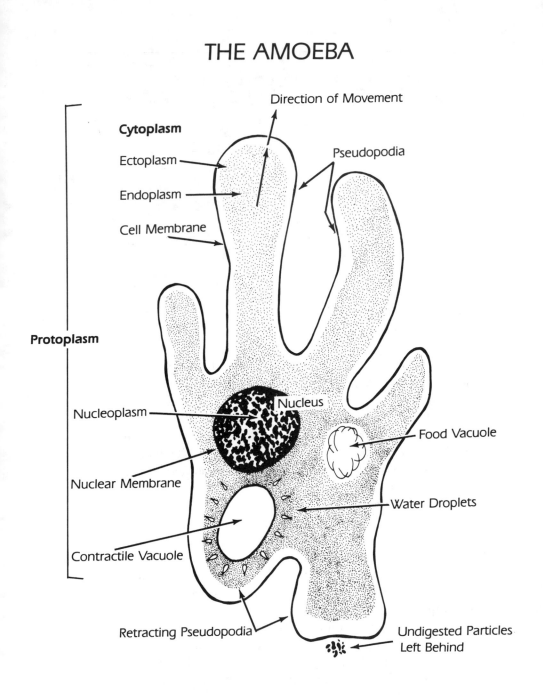

Direction of Movement

Cytoplasm

Ectoplasm

Pseudopodia

Endoplasm

Cell Membrane

Protoplasm

Nucleoplasm

Nucleus

Food Vacuole

Nuclear Membrane

Water Droplets

Contractile Vacuole

Retracting Pseudopodia

Undigested Particles
Left Behind

AMOEBA

Cells were not discovered until 1839, although life was first formed on this planet about three and a half million years ago. This is not surprising because most cells are so tiny that several million could fit into a container the size of a pencil eraser. Yet our life, our health, our path to becoming winning bodybuilders depends on the well-being of these microscopic units of life.

One of the simplest cells to study is the amoeba, a one-celled animal that is barely visible to the naked eye living in pond water. When looked at through a microscope, the amoeba reveals a basic structure similar to all living things. Like the cells in our body, it is made up of protoplasm surrounded by a cell wall or membrane and contains cytoplasm, a nucleus, and other elements vital for life.

All amoebas look approximately the same—like shapeless masses. The same is not true with human cells since we are the most complex creatures on earth. Ours have a highly organized appearance and vary in size and shape, according to their function. For example, there are three different types of muscle cells; those forming the tissue of muscles that push and pull are long and look striped; those forming the heart are similar in appearance, but much shorter; and those pushing food through the stomach and intestines are smooth and tapered. These smooth muscles function even when we are asleep or unconscious. Although body cells come in different shapes and perform different tasks, each one has certain features in common.

PROTOPLASM

Like the amoeba, every body cell is made up of protoplasm, composed mainly of hydrogen, oxygen, carbon, and nitrogen. These elements account for most of our body weight. The remainder is made up of calcium, phosphorus, chlorine, sodium, potassium, sulfur, magnesium, iron, and trace elements such as manganese, copper, and iodine. Most of these elements are chemically converted from the air we breathe and the food we eat. Carbon and hydrogen, for example, are produced chiefly from carbohydrates. Since almost everything we eat and drink undergoes a similar conversion, I would like to discuss the role of protein, fats, and carbohydrates in the cell to prepare the ground-work for a clear understanding of my nutritional programs.

CELLULAR PROTEIN

Excluding water, proteins are the most abundant substance found in the protoplasm, making up between 10 and 20 percent of the cell mass. This fact underlines the importance of eating high-quality protein, having a high rate of absorption into the body systems. Cellular protein has prime importance as a building material for the protoplasm and is divided into two types: (1) structural, holding cell structures together, such as the nuclear and cell membranes; and (2) enzymes, controlling chemical reactions in the cell.

CELLULAR LIPID OR FAT

Between 2 and 3 percent of protoplasm content is composed of lipids or fats, distributed throughout the cell, with an exceptionally high concentration in the nuclear and cell membranes. Working like guards within these membranes, lipids either allow chemicals to pass from one part of the cell to another or prevent them from doing so. Without the consent of a lipid nothing can pass the barriers. You can imagine a gate clanging shut to keep the cell safe from harm.

CELLULAR CARBOHYDRATE

Although carbohydrates average 1 percent or less of the total protoplasm mass, they play a major role in nutrition. When converted into glucose, carbohydrates are always present in the fluid surrounding each cell wall, being immediately available when needed. As glucose splits within the cell, it forms glycogen, one of the major nutrients required to release tremendous *quantities of energy.* If carbohydrates are eliminated from your diet, especially before a competitive event, your body is cut off from this essential source of energy.

IONS

Essential to life itself are the chemical reactions within the cell. These are caused by *ions,* with differing positive and negative

BODY COMPOSITION

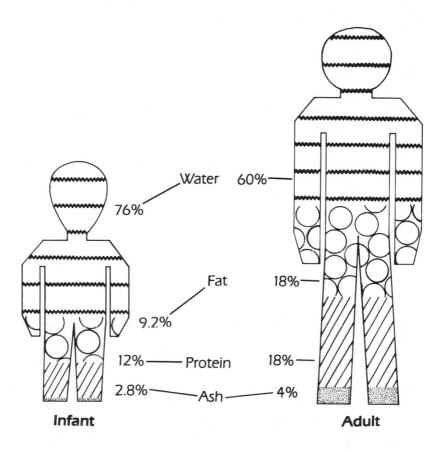

Infant   **Adult**

charges, that are found dissolved in the water of the protoplasm. Among the most important ions are potassium, magnesium, phosphate, bicarbonate, and sulfate.

CELLULAR WATER

Water causes cellular chemicals to dissolve. It makes up the largest part of the total protoplasm mass, between 70 and 75 percent. Its fluid nature allows the chemicals to move from one part of the cell to another until they are distributed evenly.

The high percentage of water in protoplasm is probably a result of life first having been created in the sea. Billions of years ago the seas were warmer than today, having been heated by erupting volcanoes and ultraviolet light, which is now screened from the earth by a layer of ozone 15 feet high. To some extent the formation of life in warm seas accounts for our body temperature, which remains between 98 and 99° F., whether the thermometer outside our window registers 120° F. or -60°. For the most part, our temperature is not affected by the type of food we eat, but by metabolic changes during the digestive process. A very hard workout can raise body temperature 1–3° F., also caused by metabolic changes as fat breaks down and more energy is burned off.

As we grow older, the amount of water, fat, protein, and minerals in our bodies changes. The water content decreases from 76 to 60 percent. Fat increases from 9.2 to 18 percent with a marked difference between men and women. Most men average 12 percent body fat, while some women may have as much as 33 percent. Protein increases slightly from 12 to 18 percent as we mature; however, it may decrease as a result of excess weight gains. Ash, a residue from minerals such as sodium, calcium, and magnesium, increases slightly from 2.8 to 5 percent.

THE CELL: THE REPRODUCTION CREW

The entire mass of protoplasm within the cell is divided into two major parts: the nucleus and a surrounding layer of cytoplasm that contains a number of elements essential to cell life. You can think of the nucleus as the boss of a crew hard at work in the cytoplasm. Members of this industrious crew include mitochondria, the energy-generating centers of the cell; ribosomes, which synthesize protein; lysosomes or waste collectors, which remove parts of the cell no longer needed; and membranes, which control the movement of particles across the cells.

Knowing what the crew is capable of doing, the nucleus directs its activities, leading to the division of the cell, a process called *mitosis,* or cell reproduction, which is constantly going on in your body, even as you sit reading these words. And it goes on every day of the year, every minute of the day; for as long as you live, some body tissues are reproducing themselves. By dividing into two parts, each with its own nucleus, each cell makes another exactly like itself. The life of a red blood cell, for example, is only 18 weeks long, yet the number in our body always remains the same.

THE CELL

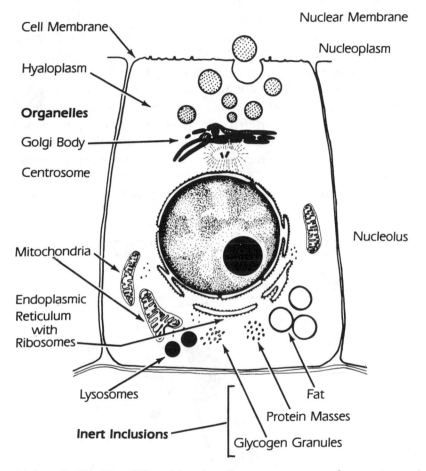

Cytoplasm

Cell Membrane

Hyaloplasm

Organelles

Golgi Body

Centrosome

Mitochondria

Endoplasmic
Reticulum
with
Ribosomes

Lysosomes

Inert Inclusions

Nucleus

Nuclear Membrane

Nucleoplasm

Nucleolus

Fat

Protein Masses

Glycogen Granules

Although 10–15 million blood cells are worn out from use each second, the same number are formed again through the process of mitosis. Cell reproduction can be seen through an electron microscope.

As far as we know, this power of a cell to divide and produce another exactly like itself exists only on Earth. It is true that stars sometimes split in two, with each half spinning away to form its own orbit. This, however, is not the formation of life, since each half is unable to produce another star.

TISSUE: A BRIDGE TO THE OUTSIDE WORLD

When a large number of similar cells are joined, they form tissue. Our body is made up of six different types: skin tissue; connective tissue, holding muscles and organs in place; blood tissue; muscle tissue; nerve tissue; and glandular tissue. Except for the tissue making up our nervous system, all can heal themselves by growing new cells. Seeing your skin heal within a few days after cutting a finger is visible proof. Of course, you also know that bones mend after being broken. The same is true of muscle tissue: after breaking down, it is quickly rebuilt by the formation of new cells.

We are most familiar with tissues involving the reaction of our five senses to a source outside the body. Light affects the tissue of our eyes; sound causes a reaction by tissues of our hearing system; the smell, taste, and quality of food stimulate the digestive tissues; objects we touch and body movement elicit a reaction from our muscular tissue.

TISSUES OF THE BODY

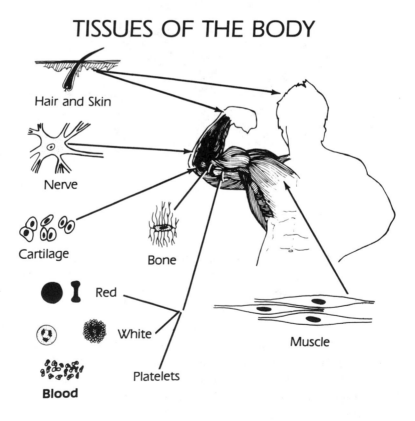

Hair and Skin

Nerve

Cartilage

Bone

Red

White

Platelets

Blood

Muscle

MAJOR ORGANS OF THE BODY

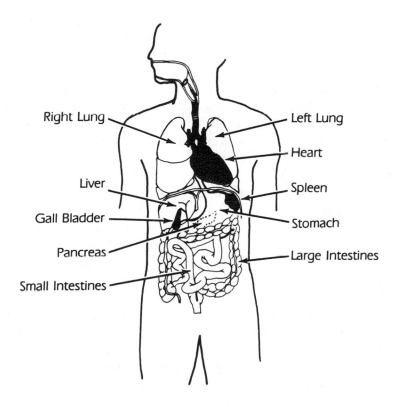

Right Lung
Left Lung
Heart
Liver
Spleen
Gall Bladder
Stomach
Pancreas
Large Intestines
Small Intestines

ORGANS THAT MAKE THE BODY FUNCTION

When a group of different tissues work together they form an organ. Your arm, for example, is composed of muscle, bone, nerve, connective, skin, and blood tissues. Your brain is also an organ, as are the liver, heart, and many other parts of the body.

A group of organs functioning together form a system. One example is the digestive system, made up of many organs, including the mouth, stomach, and intestines, all acting as parts of a unit to handle food.

In summary, cells form tissues, tissues form organs, and organs form systems that work together to create you as a unique individual. And it is the brain, the most important organ of all, that directs this entire life force within the body.

BODY SYSTEMS: HOW YOUR ORGANS WORK TOGETHER

We have now moved from looking at a cell, the smallest unit of life, to the body systems. These parts can be considered similar to the many parts of a car needed to make it run, such as the tires, fuel system, and engine. Even the best Pirelli tires will not move your car from a dead stop to traveling at 55 mph on a highway if the fuel injection system is clogged. The same holds true of your body. Each system depends on the other to keep you healthy and building a strong and muscular body.

Eight different systems work within the body. The first three mentioned below do not deal directly with food, the source of energy. The remaining five work at breaking down food so it can be transported to the cells.

Central nervous system   Controlled by the brain, the central nervous system directs every body movement. It works something like a television station receiving messages from camera or audio operators about anything seen or heard on their electronic equipment. The eyes, for example, seeing a beautiful woman, send messages to the brain describing her figure, her smile, and the color of her hair and eyes.

Muscular or locomotor system   Every body movement is accomplished by the muscular system. We can see it at work when it is being used for activities like lifting a cup, running, or lifting weights at the gym. What we can't see is that the muscles also make blood circulate and push food through the body.

Reproductive system   I have already explained the process of mitosis, which produces new body cells, but more familiar to most people is the reproductive system that gives us the birth of a child. This process is similar to mitosis once the ovum and sperm cells come together and form a zygote, which divides in two, beginning the formation of a new life.

VEGETATIVE SYSTEMS: HOW YOUR BODY PROCESSES FOOD

The following five systems are concerned directly with food, the source of energy that builds your body and keeps it in good repair. Most activities of the vegetative systems are not voluntary, but go

MAJOR ARTERIES OF THE BODY

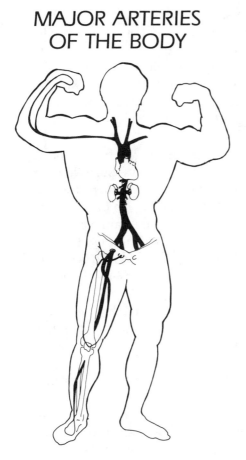

MAJOR VEINS OF THE BODY

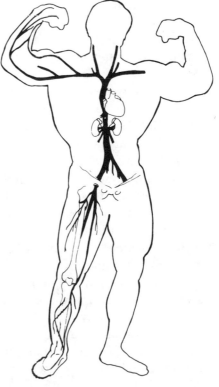

on below the level of consciousness. It is the brain, directing their activities, that makes these systems operate together so food can be chemically changed and made available to the cells.

Digestive system   Organs like the stomach and intestine are part of the digestive system, which breaks up food for absorption by the body. Since a detailed study of the digestive process is necessary for an understanding of nutrition, it will be fully discussed later.

Respiratory system   For the body to use energy from food it must combine with oxygen from the respiratory system. When we inhale, oxygen is absorbed into the bloodstream, where the red blood cells transport it to every part of the body. An exchange of nutrients and waste materials takes place where capillaries link small arteries and veins. By exhaling, we expel air not used by the body, together with carbon dioxide and water, the waste products of this conversion process. Strenuous exercise increases the conversion rate of food into energy.

Cardiovascular or circulatory system   Pumped by the heart and muscles lining blood vessels, the cardiovascular system sends blood to all parts of the body via arteries, veins, and capillaries. When food, respiratory gases, and waste materials have been chemically changed they are transported through the body using this system.

Regulating system   The endocrine glands form a regulating system that releases hormones needed for work and growth into the bloodstream. The endocrine glands also supply us with the burst of energy we need when we get excited and want to put up a good fight for something.

Excretory system   After all the useful nutrients from food have been absorbed, waste material leaves the body through the excretory system. The kidneys, for example, filter the blood and reabsorb essential substances. Other waste passing through this system includes dead blood cells, worn-out tissue, and excess vitamins and minerals.

This overall view of human physiology and biochemistry should give you an idea of how the body works as a whole, with each unit, from a cell to a system, dependent on the others. Keeping this complex, miniature universe in peak condition depends on understanding the role nutrition plays in building your body from within. In addition to discipline and a good training program, a diet designed for optimal nutrition provides the energy, bodybuilding materials, and mental alertness that give you a true competitive edge as a bodybuilder.

The following sections explore in depth the relationship between all food and drink and the body systems. The knowledge gained will eventually enable you to design a nutritional program geared specifically to your own body, temperament, and lifestyle.

THE DIGESTIVE PROCESS

We have all understood a small part of the digestive process since childhood, knowing the feeling of satisfying hunger by having a meal. Certainly, most of us are familiar with the discomfort of overeating and have complained of being bloated for hours after eating a holiday dinner. The same feeling can accompany an allergic reaction to certain foods because they are digested improperly, remaining in the stomach for an extended period of time before passing through the intestinal system.

When empty, the stomach is approximately the size of two fists placed close together, yet it expands according to the amount of food you eat. Digestion of the average dinner takes 1–1½ days, while a Thanksgiving dinner with all the trimmings will take 2½–3 days. In general, four or five small meals, as recommended in many of my diets, are digested more completely than the habitual three square meals a day.

ENZYMES: THE WONDER CHEMICALS OF LIFE

Although food satisfies feelings of hunger, it is useless to the body until it undergoes a chemical change and enters the bloodstream. This process is governed by complex proteins called *enzymes,* often referred to as the wonder chemicals of life. Without thousands of them at work in the body, you would be unable to digest food, build bones and tissue, and remove waste through the excretory system. Enzymes are delicate but powerful. In a laboratory chemists break down protein molecules into amino acids by adding a strong acid solution to the protein and boiling it for approximately 24 hours. Your body enzymes accomplish the same thing in less than 3 hours without strong acids at normal body temperature.

PROTEIN METABOLISM

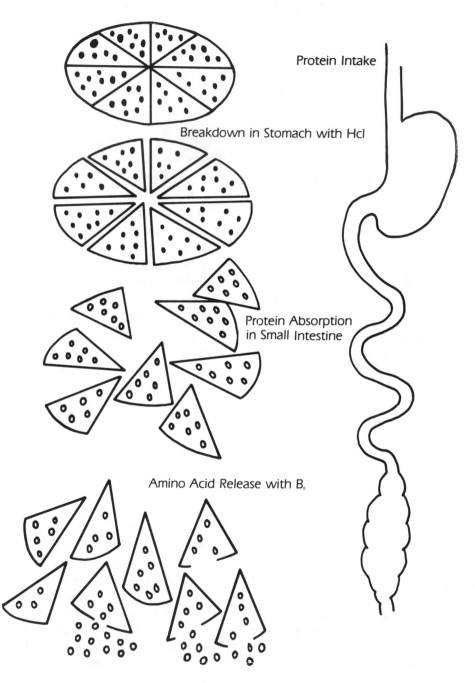

Protein Intake

Breakdown in Stomach with Hcl

Protein Absorption
in Small Intestine

Amino Acid Release with B$_6$

Enzymes are found in all living things, being used by fireflies to glow in the dark and by silkworms to work free of their cocoons. Enzymes in yeast make bread rise and turn grape juice into wine, wine into vinegar, and milk into cheese. Also, they are specific. Those capable of breaking down proteins are unable to break down fats or carbohydrates. A different group of enzymes converts fat into fatty acids and glycerol, and still another is needed to break down starches and complex sugars into simple sugars. Since each enzyme reacts to a specific class of food, it is best not to combine too many types of food at one meal to ensure proper digestion and full utilization of the nutrients in food. When you eat food the body can use efficiently, it will not show up as a weight increase.

The enzymes in your body control the *speed* of all chemical changes, but the enzymes themselves never change, simply serving as catalysts to make something happen while they remain the same. This unique property of enzymes can be understood more clearly by drawing a parallel: Suppose you wanted to walk a distance of 100 miles, but after realizing this would take 20–24 hours, you took a bus instead. The same distance would be covered in 2 hours, and after speeding up your trip the bus would remain unchanged. So it is with the thousands of enzymes in your body, accelerating the breakdown of food in the intestinal tract. Some enzymes need a trace of other substances, called *coenzymes,* to help convert food into substances that can be absorbed by the body. Vitamins play an essential role in producing many of the coenzymes required to maintain a chemical balance in the body systems.

THE DIGESTIVE TRACT

The digestive enzymes are active in the mouth, stomach, pancreas, and walls of the small intestine. Food is first acted on by water and ptyalin, an enzyme produced by the salivary glands in the mouth. It is here that the conversion of carbohydrates into simple sugars originates. Ptyalin mixes with the food being ground between our teeth and breaks apart large starch molecules into small molecules of simple sugar.

After being chewed, the food passes down the esophagus to the stomach, where it mixes with gastric juices containing the enzyme

PASSAGE OF FOOD THROUGH DIGESTIVE TRACT

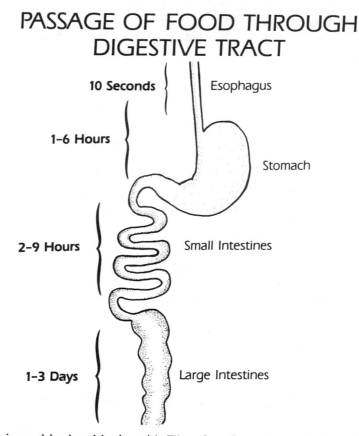

10 Seconds — Esophagus

1-6 Hours

Stomach

2-9 Hours — Small Intestines

1-3 Days — Large Intestines

pepsin and hydrochloric acid. The digestion of protein is activated by pepsin, which needs an acid medium to release its full potency. For this reason I have recommended hydrochloric acid tablets in many of the suggested diets to maintain the normal condition of the stomach, which is definitely on the acidic side. Ordinary meals will pass through the stomach to the small intestine in three or four hours, while substances that are watery, like soups and juices, pass through quickly. Carbohydrate substances leave the stomach first and are followed by the proteins. Fats remain for the longest time, accounting for the feeling of fullness after eating meals high in fat content.

When the partially digested food leaves the stomach it enters the small intestine, where the main absorption of nutrients takes place. It is first acted on by the pancreas, a gland located just beneath the stomach that manufactures and secretes juices containing some of the body's most important digestive enzymes. Amylase completes the digestion of starch molecules begun by the enzyme ptyalin in the mouth; lipases split fats; and proteases continue the digestion of proteins begun by pepsin in the stomach.

The absorption of nutrients is accomplished by millions of villi, fingerlike projections lining the intestinal walls. Each one has a miniature, complete blood system with an artery carrying blood in and a vein carrying it out. As food is digested, villi pick up the particles and pass them into the veins. During this process food is converted into nutrients capable of being absorbed into the bloodstream. Carbohydrates are converted into glucose and fructose, fats become fatty acids, and protein is broken down into amino acids. Dietary vitamins in food are absorbed with water and fat, while minerals found in food are absorbed with water. The only nutrients not requiring digestion are vitamin and mineral supplements and some types of sugar, such as glucose. Because their chemical structure is elementary, they do not undergo chemical changes but are dissolved by fluids in the digestive tract and pass directly into the bloodstream. Only alcohol is absorbed directly through the stomach walls. Any products left undigested

ACTION AND SOURCES OF DIGESTIVE JUICES

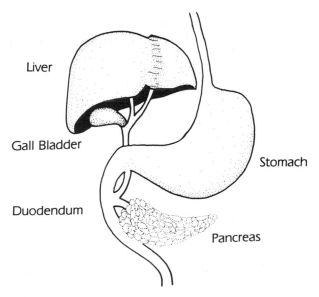

Liver

Gall Bladder

Stomach

Duodendum

Pancreas

enter the large intestine. Since digestive enzymes are not secreted here, no change occurs except for the absorption of water through the intestinal walls.

Although the liver has a number of different enzymes at work, they do not convert nutrients for absorption into the bloodstream as mentioned above. Instead they help the liver to manufacture products needed by the individual cells and to store glycogen and the fat-soluble vitamins A and D. The liver also serves to detoxify a number of substances and allows them to enter the bloodstream as harmless chemicals. One of its major functions involves its relation to the gallbladder, which holds bile, producing salts that allow for the efficient digestion of fats.

This discussion of the passage of food through the digestive tract makes obvious the chemical complexity of any meal containing protein, fats, and carbohydrates. Everything you eat must undergo a process of conversion into simple chemical products that can be absorbed through the intestinal walls and transported by your bloodstream to each individual cell. Only then are digested nutrients turned into the materials needed for building muscle tissue and for energy to meet the rigorous demands of a body-builder in hard training.

Keep in mind that the process of digestion is inhibited if you are eating in a hurry or in a nervous state of mind. Avoid combining more than one type of protein in a single meal as well as too many different types of food. The more you can do to increase the efficiency of the digestive process—eat, without stress, foods that don't stress the organs of digestion—the more you can improve the results of a proper nutrition program.

3
BASIC NUTRIENTS

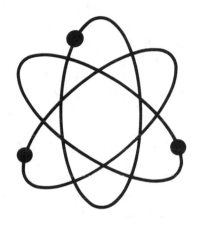

The chemicals found in your body are almost like those found in food. Both consist of at least 18 elements and probably as many as 40. These are made up of combinations of atoms, such as carbon, hydrogen, oxygen, nitrogen, calcium, potassium, and phosphorus. Some compounds are necessary for building and repairing tissues, others protect the body from disease, and others provide energy and warmth.

A stream of nutrient chemicals formed from digested food flows continuously into our cells, providing the energy needed to train, work, play, make love, and even sit in a chair watching television. When the cells have used the amount of nutrients required for fuel each day, any excess is stored in the tissues. Your body can store a limited supply of carbohydrates and an almost unlimited amount of fat, but protein cannot be stored. It must be provided by your intake of food with the amount absorbed by the body being dependent on the quality of protein you eat.

PROTEIN: BODYBUILDING FOOD

Without protein, there would be no life since it forms the basic substance of our muscles, bones, brain, nerves, heart, and every other organ. Only protein contains nitrogen, an essential part of protoplasm. Without it, the cells would slowly wear away, unable to reproduce and form new cells. As previously mentioned, red blood cells have a life of only 18 weeks and must constantly be replaced. Without a supply of dietary protein providing the amino acids essential for the reproduction of new cells, this would be impossible. The same holds true for cells lining the intestine, which are renewed every 1½ days. The synthesis of protein is also essential for *anabolism,* or the formation of new tissue, occurring at an even rate for the average person that is stepped up considerably with bodybuilders since they are continuously training, breaking down tissue, and building muscle mass. Dietary protein is also essential to *catabolism,* a process through which the amino acids found only in protein are broken down, thereby liberating energy. Again, this would occur at an even rate for those not in intensive training but accelerates for bodybuilders and other athletes due to their increased expenditure of energy.

Proteins also serve a regulatory role in forming enzymes that trigger all chemical reactions in the body. The body is protected from infectious diseases by antibodies composed of proteins. And hormones like insulin that regulate our daily processes are also derived from our daily intake of protein.

All protein foods are not equally efficient. Their value is based on the type of amino acids they contain, which combine with nitrogen and form thousands of different proteins necessary to build and repair cellular tissue. This takes place during digestion when hydrochloric acid and enzymes break down the intact protein molecule into amino acids so they can be absorbed through the intestinal wall. Of 22 known amino acids, 13 can be produced by the body, synthesized by glands like the liver. These—alanine, arginine, asparagine, aspartic acid, cysteine, cystine, glucine, glutamic acid, glutamine, hydroxyproline, proline, serine, and tyrosine—are called *nonessential amino acids.* They can safely be omitted when enough nitrogen and other nutrients are supplied. *Essential amino acids,* used for building tissue and other functions just discussed, cannot be made by the body but must be taken directly from our daily intake of food. They are histidine, isoleucine, leucine, lysine, methionine, phenylalanine, threonine, tryptophan, and valine. Those who are vegetarians should be aware that one amino acid cannot replace another.

When food contains the essential amino acids it is considered a complete protein. With the exception of soybeans, all complete proteins are derived from animal sources: meat, fish, eggs, poultry, cheese, and milk. Although most gelatin comes from an animal source, it does not fall into this category because it lacks the necessary amino acids. Protein foods derived from plants are considered incomplete since they lack the amino acids essential for building tissue and repairing the body. Certain plant foods, like rice, potatoes, nuts, breads, and grain cereals, contain the essential amino acids but in lesser quantities than animal foods. Many cereals and rice are low in lysine, while dry beans, peanuts, and brewer's yeast are low in methionine. It would be necessary to eat a pound of potatoes to provide the necessary amino acids found in only an ounce of meat. Keep in mind that the amino acids of most animal proteins are absorbed efficiently, their rate ranging from 90 to 95 percent, while the digestibility of some plant proteins may be as low as 73 percent. Vegetarians also run the risk of miscombining vegetable proteins and thus failing to form complete proteins containing all the essential amino acids. The growth and reproduction of cells demand that all the essential amino acids be ingested at the same time in the same meal. A missing amino acid cannot be supplied several hours later and still find the essential ones waiting to be assembled into a complete protein before being digested. Eggs are a prime example of a complete protein, containing *all* of the essential amino acids in *sufficient* amounts to maintain life and support growth.

The digestion of protein begins in the stomach and is completed in the small intestine. Enzymes from the pancreas actually cause the breakdown of the protein you eat into amino acids. Following this, they are absorbed from the intestine and distributed to the body cells through the bloodstream. When more protein is eaten than needed for the functions mentioned at the beginning of this section, the excess is metabolized for energy. If your diet contains insufficient carbohydrates needed for energy, your body will draw on the protein vital to building body tissue. As mentioned earlier, this is a mistake many bodybuilders continue making, particularly before competition when they need to be in top form.

PROTEIN POWDERS

Another danger comes from depending on protein powders, tablets, and liquids to supply major nutritional elements. Many bodybuilders using these concentrates believe advertisements that promote them as highly concentrated food products. Remember, it takes very little muscular weight to write an advertisement but a great deal to lift weights and train hard. Seeing 90 percent protein written on the label gives the impression that the stuff inside the can originates from a more valuable protein source than eggs, fish, poultry, or meat. However, this does not necessarily mean that 90 percent of the powder is protein. For example, a can weighing two pounds may contain one pound of pure protein, 90 percent of which has a nutrient value. The remaining pound consists of other ingredients added to stabilize the protein and prevent it from spoiling. At present, the average protein content of most brands ranges between 40 and 70 percent; some higher-quality products might supply as much as 65–75 percent.

Even so, an important difference should be noted between protein from animal sources and protein in powdered concentrates, tablets, and fruit- and chocolate-flavored liquids. I have come to define the first as *live protein* and the second as *dead protein* based on the condition of DNA molecules found in the cells. These molecules work as an information center, having the codes and blueprints necessary to assemble hundreds of different proteins needed by the body. Each day they send out thousands of messages on building and repairing tissue. The DNA in animal protein, even when the animal is slaughtered, remains alive and unbroken. In the case of protein powders from animal sources, however, the DNA is broken down during the manufacturing process, and its ability to build body tissue is impaired.

Also, the protein in concentrates is not absorbed into the bloodstream to the same extent as is dietary protein. This point is one of the chief considerations in the selection of high-quality protein in the bodybuilder's diet. The fillers and waste products contained in the concentrates contain substances that inhibit enzyme action in the digestive tract, resulting in effective utilization of the protein. For example, in comparing 4 grams of protein from an egg yolk with an equal weight of powdered protein, you will absorb about 3½ grams of protein from the egg, but less than

2 from the powder. Therefore, concentrates should never be considered substitutes for fresh food, most particularly from animal sources. Any dependency on them can only set you on the road downhill as a competitive bodybuilder.

Those who are underweight may gain an advantage by taking the powders as a pick-me-up between meals, perhaps using them to spare protein needed for building muscles, but not to replace eggs, fish, meat, or poultry. Then it is best mixed with milk or water rather than fruit juice, since the high concentration of sugar does not combine well with protein and may putrefy in the colon without being digested.

PROTEIN UTILIZATION: HOW MUCH IS ABSORBED

As a bodybuilder, you must consider the net protein utilization (NPU) or rate of protein absorption into the bloodstream. For those who are trying to shed pounds this should be highlighted because some meat items are much higher in fat than others. For example, beef and chicken both have an absorption rate of 68 percent, yet chicken has the advantage of easier digestibility and contains almost half the calories of an equal weight of beef, pork, or lamb.

The protein utilization rate of some common foods follows.

FOOD	NPU
Eggs	88%
Fish	78%
Dairy products	76%
Meat	68%
Soybeans	48%
Natural brown rice	40%
Red beans	39%
Coconut	38%
Nuts	35%
White beans	33%
Maize	25%
Whole wheat bread	21%
White bread	20%

The average person needs a daily quote of 1 gram of protein for every kilogram (2.2 pounds) of body weight. Adult males should consume 75–100 grams per day; however, an extra allowance of protein is required to build muscular weight for those in heavy training. The food intake tables found at the end of this chapter were calculated to accommodate both male and female bodybuilders whose goals range widely from training for good health and a vigorous appearance to entering competition at championship levels. My own intake of protein is high due to a schedule of heavy weight training, so I always take care to choose the best sources. In addition to eating only prime cuts of meat and making a point of having fresh fish, I also include eggs in my daily food intake since they have the highest protein utilization rate, as noted above.

When the consumption of protein is increased, the body does not automatically secrete more hydrochloric acid (HCl) to aid digestion. Therefore, if you are in heavy training and have increased your intake of protein, it may be necessary to take HCl and digestive enzyme supplements. The role of enzymes during the digestive process is discussed in greater detail later. Most importantly, you must learn to judge what is best for your own body because it is essential to the learning process, and you learn to see yourself as a unique individual, a point of great value when you are in competition, standing on that stage and posing for the judges and the crowd.

Protein foods from animal and plant sources are listed in the appendix. Study these charts carefully, particularly noting the fat content of different food items. Those having problems with excess weight should select items high in protein but low in fat. For instance, there is little difference between the protein content of sirloin and round steaks, yet sirloin contains approximately 2½ times more fat. Bear in mind that not all fat in meat is visible and that some cuts may contain over 40 percent fat even if you have been very careful to trim it off before beginning to eat. Hamburgers sold in fast food chains have a notoriously high fat content, which may be the reason you feel more satisfied after eating one out than after eating one at home. Being more difficult to digest, fat remains in the stomach longer and gives a feeling of being full for an extended period of time.

Regarding foods from plant sources, keep in mind that only soybeans contain a significant amount of essential amino acids, but their balance is not the same as that found in meat, eggs, and fish. Since they have a limited amount of methionine, one of the essential amino acids, more grams of soybeans than meat are needed to furnish the complete proteins necessary for building muscle tissue.

If a favorite fruit or vegetable is not listed with protein foods, refer to the tables of carbohydrates in the appendix. Many produce items contain less than 3 grams of protein, so they cannot be considered an efficient source of this nutrient.

Be advised that I do not recommend all foods listed in the tables, but many popular food items are given, so you may see my reasons for excluding them from my diet programs. Frozen, breaded fishsticks, for example, do not meet my requirements for high-quality protein, no matter what the manufacturer has chosen to claim on the label. Fresh food in its most natural form always takes first place. Also, it is doubtful if an 8-ounce package of fish sticks actually contains 38 grams of protein from the fish itself. More likely, a high percentage of this amount comes from substances used for breading. The tables are intended mainly to provide an awareness of protein sources, and my preferences are stated clearly throughout the book.

In summary, the best bodybuilding foods from animal sources are fish, meat, eggs, and poultry. Dairy products like cheese are high in protein but also in fat, which tends to form fat deposits under the skin, causing a loss of definition. The best foods from plant sources are beans, nuts, seeds, and grain products.

CARBOHYDRATES: PRIMARY SOURCE OF ENERGY

Common among bodybuilders is the practice of going on diets high in protein and very low in carbohydrate. Their understanding of the essential role played by protein in building muscle and repairing tissue is certainly correct. Yet too many remain unaware that carbohydrates are needed to power those muscles and to generate energy needed for training. Remember, the energy needs of the body take priority over all other functions, and when you do not have sufficient carbohydrates in the diet to provide energy it will be taken from the protein needed to build tissue. For this reason, many bodybuilders enter competitions in sad shape.

A similar mistake might be made by someone who put his heart and soul into building a racing car with the intention of winning the Grand Prix. "It's the finest car ever made," he would say, talking with pride about the cylinders as some talk about their biceps or lats. His fascination with the car's styling and mechanics might cause him to lose sight of the fact that only a pint of gas was in the fuel tank when he hit the race track in competition for the Grand Prix. You and I know his chances of winning, no matter how masterfully the car was engineered or how finely tuned the engine. And so it is with those who work hard on muscular development and then neglect carbohydrates, the body's fuel and primary source of energy.

A great deal of this problem may arise from a mistaken understanding of the sources of carbohydrates. True, donuts, pies, cakes, ice cream, pastry, and other such items and snack foods are loaded with carbohydrates. But none of these should be used to provide your source of carbohydrates. Instead they should come primarily from fresh fruits and vegetables and secondarily from whole grain products, nuts, and seeds. Keep a careful eye on the caloric content of these last items because many are high in fat content.

Some bodybuilders hope to compensate for a drastically reduced amount of carbohydrate in their diet by taking vitamin and mineral supplements. But vitamins and minerals are not sources of energy, they serve *supporting* roles in its use and conservation. For example, vitamin C taken when training builds resistance against colds, calcium increases muscle function, and B-complex vitamins are necessary for normal functioning of the liver and nervous system. Obviously, they are all important, but none can provide the energy received from eating fresh fruits, vegetables, and whole grain products.

Unlike protein, for which the process of digestion begins in the stomach, the digestion of starch in carbohydrates begins in the mouth and then continues in the small intestine. The main product of carbohydrate metabolism is glucose, commonly known as *blood sugar*. In this form it enters our bloodstream and first supplies the energy needs of our central nervous system. Any glucose not used immediately is stored in the liver or muscles as glycogen; the rest becomes fat tissue. As bodybuilders, we must be concerned with our glycogen reserve because this is the primary fuel of hardworking muscles, and the supply of it is limited.

The body can store only a limited supply of glycogen: approximately 350 grams when the supply is at its peak with one-third of the amount held in the liver and the remainder in the muscles. Liver glycogen is available for immediate use, being quickly converted into glucose when needed by the body. Muscle glycogen, however, does not have the necessary enzymes for this direct conversion into body fuel but furnishes glucose indirectly. When the muscle contracts, glycogen is converted into lactic acid, which is carried in the bloodstream to the liver and then converted into glycogen or glucose as needed by the body. For this reason, it does not reach the brain and nervous system as directly as liver glycogen.

The reserve of glycogen lasts 2–15 hours, depending on your activities. Someone playing checkers can have enough to last most of the day, while bodybuilders in heavy training can use their entire supply of glycogen within 2–3 hours. The body will then switch to alternate but less efficient performance fuels. Amino acids, for instance, can be converted by the liver into glucose in order to keep the brain and nerves supplied with fuel. This puts an unnecessary stress on the liver and drains the supply of amino acids needed for building muscles and repairing the body.

Because peak performance depends on the optimum use of body fuel, I stress training on alternate days when exercise programs require intensive workouts. If you train for two or three hours on Monday, you should not train again on Tuesday. After a heavy workout it takes about 48 hours to restore the full amount of glycogen, and you cannot train properly without it. Most professional athletes are aware of this and do not play the day before competitive matches so they can draw from a full supply of energy on the following day. I have known many bodybuilders who suffer a high degree of tension and irritability without realizing their body is in a state of chemical imbalance caused by the lack of carbohydrates that supply glucose to the nervous system. They cannot hope to make up for this lack by gulping down vitamin or mineral tablets since they do not contain glycogen needed to release glucose.

It is natural carbohydrates from fresh fruits and vegetables that are needed on a regular basis to replenish energy for the nervous system, which becomes highly irritated without sufficient glucose to meet its needs. Refined carbohydrates like sugar are so concentrated that they overload body systems equipped to store only a limited amount for energy needs. Cake, pie, candy, and soda pop cause the blood sugar level to rise. Your body responds by producing insulin, a hormone effecting a rapid drop in the blood sugar level. The release of too much insulin is always a shock to the body, and the seesaw rising and lowering of blood sugar levels wreaks havoc with the nervous system, causing a certain loss of stability. Just think of this next time you reach for a candy bar. It is carbohydrates from fresh fruits that provide the best energy source. By eating an apple, pear, or grapes before going to the gym you will raise your energy level because the liver synthesizes fruit at a slow but continuous pace, keeping blood sugar at a constant level.

By consuming carbohydrates 30–60 minutes before going to the gym to train, you also prevent their conversion into fat, which gives you the smooth look that bodybuilders take great pains to avoid. Keep in mind that carbohydrates and proteins serve two different functions, and their need varies according to your training schedule, weight, and competitive goals. Because protein builds tissue on a continuous basis, whether you are awake or asleep, it must be included in the daily diet even if you are not training. On the other hand, the need for carbohydrates changes according to the drain on glycogen reserves, making it far greater when you train than on days between workouts. The same principle is applied when getting gas for your car: a full tank is needed for a 300-mile drive but only half a tank for 150 miles. And those who eliminate carbohydrates entirely run the risk of excessive breakdown of tissue protein, loss of sodium, and involuntary dehydration.

Summing up, carbohydrates serve as a high-performance fuel, furnishing energy for the brain, nervous system, and the hardworking muscles of bodybuilders and all endurance athletes. The best sources are fresh fruits and vegetables, followed by whole grain products like breads and some cereals. Dried fruits contain a high percentage of sugar and should be avoided by those who are trying to lose weight. I particularly recommend grapes, pears, or apples before going to the gym. By reserving your intake of high-calorie carbohydrates for the period before a heavy workout, you will prevent them from being stored as fat, allowing them to burn off as needed for energy.

FAT: SECONDARY SOURCE OF ENERGY

Competitive bodybuilders consider fat their worst enemy because it forms in layers between muscle and skin, causing a loss of definition. Many years ago, when bodybuilding was in its beginning stages, definition was not a deciding factor in winning competitions. At that time, building huge muscles was very difficult to accomplish, so a man with enormous muscle size was usually declared the winner of contests. This accounts for the pictures taken of bodybuilders many years ago, which show men huge in proportion but with little thought given to form and balancing the body. However, as gaining bulk became easier over the years, definition and the rigid discipline it required came to the forefront and evolved into the deciding factor for winning competitions.

Because body fat interferes with the striations that should be seen between muscles or groups of muscles, it should be kept at a low percentage of body weight. Yet, some dietary fat is necessary to stay healthy. This does not mean adding butter to vegetables or eating bacon for breakfast to maintain a chemical balance of nutrients in your body. Some fat is found in almost all food. A cup of spinach, for example, contains .3 grams, an insignificant amount, while 8 ounces of porterhouse steak contains approximately 78 grams—more than enough fat to meet the daily nutritional requirements of those not doing hard physical work. Always keep in mind that 100 grams of fat (about 3½ ounces) contain 900 calories, while the same weight of protein or carbohydrate food contains only 400. The average American male consumes over 150 grams of fat daily, enjoying the feeling of having eaten a satisfying meal because fat and food fried in it take much longer to digest than protein prepared simply. Unlike competitive athletes, many people are controlled by their appetites rather than the goal of building a healthy, vigorous body. Others are not aware that many harmless-looking foods contain a high percentage of fat. A Brazil nut, for example contains 67 percent, sunflower seeds contain 47 percent, and most cheese contains 30 percent fat.

Fats or lipids are similar to other nutrients in that they perform a number of functions essential to keeping body systems in harmony. They serve as a concentrated source of energy because one gram contains nine calories, while the same amount of protein or carbohydrates has only four. In other words, body fat has more than twice the amount of stored energy as the glycogen in our muscle tissue. Glycogen has the advantage of burning better in the short-term maximum sport loads required for lifting weights and bodybuilding. Having all of our energy reserves in the form of muscle glycogen seems like a fine idea. But remember, each gram has less than half the energy value of fat; therefore, twice as much would be needed and would result in an unacceptable burden of extra weight.

In addition to serving as a source of energy, fat is needed to form normal tissue, being used by the cells for repair and reproduction. It is found in every organ but the brain and parts of the nervous system, although they too contain substances similar to fat that are formed from proteins and carbohydrates. Fat acts as a protective device by surrounding the kidneys, heart, and liver and helping to anchor them in place. It even cushions the eyeball from the impact of car accidents and brutal blows delivered to the head in some sports. By functioning as a carrier for the fat-soluble vitamins A, D, E, and K, it permits their absorption into the bloodstream and their storage for future use. Our bodies are insulated from temperature changes by the same layer of fat that gives well-proportioned women those luscious contours appreciated by men.

Fats are digested in a different manner from either carbohydrates or protein. They must be mixed with bile so enzymes from the pancreas and intestine can act on them. They are stored as body fat only when more is absorbed than can be used immediately. If eaten alone, they are digested much more slowly than other nutrients; without the accompaniment of proteins or carbohydrates, they are not completely digested. In this case a residue is left that is liable to become toxic and cause headaches, intestinal gas, or loss of appetite. Excess body fat not only leads to obesity but overworks the heart and cardiovascular system, while the additional weight places stress on every joint and major bone in the body.

Those bodybuilders who tend to bulk up and then crash-diet before competing should be aware of constantly putting their body under the stress just mentioned. And even worse, by bulking up, they increase both muscle and fat with the greater percentage of the gain composed of fat. When they start cutting down, the fat cells still remain, being very difficult to displace after having formed. Fat disappears only when training very rapidly with a minimum break between sets and none between reps. I have always made a point of keeping fat at a low level throughout the year, thus gaining the advantage of maintaining top form without the necessity of crash-dieting. For this reason, my energy level is constant, and I have spared my nervous system the shock that results from the drastic change of bulking up and cutting down.

To summarize, fats are a concentrated source of energy needed to carry fat-soluble vitamins. They contain more than double the number of calories of protein and carbohydrates; therefore, your daily intake of them should be kept at a low level. The most common sources are butter, margarine, oil, mayonnaise, nuts, bacon, and fatty meats. Whole milk, eggs, chocolate, and avocados naturally contain some fat.

WATER

Water is rarely regarded as an essential nutrient, yet it ranks after oxygen as the most important element necessary for life. While a healthy person can live for weeks without food, he could not survive longer than a few days without water. Over three-fourths of our weight is composed of water, which in the average adult body amounts to more than 40 quarts. Working as a solvent for all products of digestion, it holds food, vitamins, and minerals in solution so they can pass through intestinal walls into the bloodstream for use throughout the body. It also transports and removes all wastes, regulates body temperature, and helps prevent constipation.

Bodybuilders should be aware that sufficient water in our body systems is essential to maintaining a proper balance of electrolytes, such as potassium, sodium, magnesium, and calcium. When dissolved in water, these minerals conduct electric currents through the nervous system to the brain and *signal muscle contraction.* Dehydration can upset the chemical balance of electrolytes and result in weakened muscles and exhaustion.

Most adults lose approximately three quarts of water daily through perspiration and excretion. Of course, this rate is much higher with hardworking athletes who sweat heavily and is increased even more when exercising on hot and humid days. This is when many athletes fall prey to heat exhaustion, evidenced by a headache, weakness, muscle cramps, heavy sweating, and pale, clammy skin. When you become dehydrated the cells also become dehydrated, impairing their ability to build tissue and utilize energy efficiently. Without enough water, toxic elements build up in the bloodstream, you don't sweat, and blood volume decreases so you transport less oxygen and nutrients through your body.

And again, the result is fatigue and weakened muscles.

Replace lost fluids with water, not soft drinks. Flavored sodas, as you well know, are high in calories and artificial flavorings. Those labeled *dietetic* contain chemicals that cause an unhealthy retention of water. In addition, your stomach will absorb about 70 percent of one glass of water, but only 6 percent of the same amount of a cola or other soft drink.

From 8 to 10 glasses of water are recommended for the average person, but when exercising you need far more fluids. While training for competition I drank a great deal of water, especially while training in the gym. The consumption of extra vitamins, proteins, or alcohol also requires extra water.

A point of information for those who drink only distilled water for its purity. During the process of distilling the water to kill all bacteria and other contaminants, all minerals are also removed.

DAILY INTAKE OF PROTEIN, CARBOHYDRATES, AND FAT

The intake tables that follow are meant only to serve as a guide for your daily intake of food. The total amount of calories is not as important as paying careful attention to the breakdown of proteins, carbohydrates, and fat. Exact figures in grams and calories are not given because each person is an individual with a different rate of metabolism affecting the utilization of food. For example, bodybuilders who normally weigh over 240 pounds have a slower rate of metabolism compared to others 50 pounds lighter. Those weighing less than 150 pounds usually have a faster than normal rate of metabolism.

Unless you are extremely well acquainted with the way your body adapts to diets for gaining or losing weight, start with the lower figures on the intake tables. Then work upward until you reach the combination of protein, carbohydrates, and fats that works best for you. Many will find this is an ideal method to avoid gaining weight while adjusting their intake of nutrients to suit individual needs.

Bear in mind that fat intake shown on the charts merely indicates the amount you *may* need. Adding fat to the diets listed later in the book is unnecessary since fat is found in all animal food, including eggs, fish, and meat, and in trace amounts in fruits and vegetables.

AVERAGE MALE BODYBUILDER TRAINING UP TO 1 HOUR, 5-6 TIMES A WEEK, FOR MAINTAINING WEIGHT

MINIMUM REQUIRED DAILY INTAKE OF PROTEIN, CARBOHYDRATES, AND FAT

Body Weight		Protein		Carbohydrates		Fat	
KILOGRAMS	POUNDS	GRAMS	CALORIES	GRAMS	CALORIES	GRAMS	CALORIES
40-45	90-100	40-50	160-200	180-300	720-1200	30-40	270-360
45-55	100-120	45-60	180-240	200-300	800-1200	35-45	315-405
55-68	120-150	60-80	240-320	220-330	880-1320	40-50	360-450
68-77	150-170	70-90	280-360	240-350	960-1400	45-55	405-495
77-86	170-190	80-100	320-400	250-360	1000-1440	40-60	450-540
86-95	190-210	90-110	360-440	265-280	1060-1120	55-65	495-485
over 95	over 210	110-115	400-460	270-285	1080-1140	55-70	495-630

NONCOMPETITIVE MALE BODYBUILDER TRAINING 1-2 HOURS, 3-6 TIMES A WEEK, FOR LONG-TERM MUSCLE GAIN

MINIMUM REQUIRED DAILY INTAKE OF PROTEIN, CARBOHYDRATES, AND FAT

Body Weight		Protein		Carbohydrates		Fat	
KILOGRAMS	POUNDS	GRAMS	CALORIES	GRAMS	CALORIES	GRAMS	CALORIES
40-45	90-100	50-60	200-240	150-165	600-660	20-40	180-360
45-55	100-120	55-65	220-260	170-200	680-800	30-50	270-450
55-68	120-150	65-75	260-300	200-240	800-960	30-50	270-450
68-77	150-170	75-90	300-360	210-250	840-1000	30-50	270-450
77-86	170-190	85-100	340-400	220-270	880-1080	30-50	270-450
86-95	190-210	95-110	380-440	250-270	1000-1080	35-50	270-450
Over 95	Over 210	100-120	400-480	250-280	1000-1120	30-50	270-450

COMPETITIVE MALE BODYBUILDER TRAINING 2 HOURS, 6 TIMES A WEEK, FOR QUICK FAT LOSS AND MUSCLE GAIN

MINIMUM REQUIRED DAILY INTAKE OF PROTEIN, CARBOHYDRATES, AND FAT

Body Weight		Protein		Carbohydrates		Fat	
KILOGRAMS	POUNDS	GRAMS	CALORIES	GRAMS	CALORIES	GRAMS	CALORIES
40-45	90-100	60-75	240-300	65-80	260-320	10-30	90-270
45-55	100-120	70-85	280-340	70-90	280-360	10-30	90-270
55-68	120-150	80-95	320-380	80-100	320-400	10-30	90-270
68-77	150-170	90-110	360-480	90-120	360-480	15-35	135-315
77-86	170-190	100-120	400-430	100-130	400-520	15-35	135-315
86-95	190-210	105-125	420-500	110-130	440-520	10-30	90-270
over 95	over 210	110-130	440-520	110-125	440-500	10-30	90-270

AVERAGE FEMALE BODYBUILDER TRAINING UP TO 1 HOUR, 5-6 TIMES A WEEK, TO MAINTAIN WEIGHT

MINIMUM REQUIRED DAILY INTAKE OF PROTEIN, CARBOHYDRATES, AND FAT

Body Weight		Protein		Carbohydrates		Fat	
KILOGRAMS	POUNDS	GRAMS	CALORIES	GRAMS	CALORIES	GRAMS	CALORIES
40-45	90-100	40-50	160-200	180-210	720-840	30-35	270-315
45-55	100-120	50-55	200-220	180-220	740-880	35-40	315-360
55-68	120-150	60-70	240-280	210-230	840-920	40-45	360-405
68-77	150-170	65-75	260-300	240-280	960-1120	45-50	405-450
77-86	170-190	75-90	300-360	250-300	1000-1200	50-55	450-495
86-95	190-210	85-95	340-380	265-320	1060-1280	53-57	477-513
over 95	over 210	90-100	360-400	280-340	1120-1360	55-60	495-540

NONCOMPETITIVE FEMALE BODYBUILDER TRAINING 1-2 HOURS, 3-6 TIMES A WEEK, FOR LONG-TERM MUSCLE GAIN

MINIMUM REQUIRED DAILY INTAKE OF PROTEIN, CARBOHYDRATES, AND FAT

Body Weight		Protein		Carbohydrates		Fat	
KILOGRAMS	POUNDS	GRAMS	CALORIES	GRAMS	CALORIES	GRAMS	CALORIES
40-45	90-100	60-70	240-280	165-180	660-720	10-30	90-270
45-55	100-120	65-75	260-300	170-190	680-770	10-30	90-270
55-68	120-150	80-90	320-360	200-210	800-840	10-30	90-270
68-77	150-170	85-95	340-380	210-230	840-920	15-40	135-360
77-86	170-190	95-105	380-420	220-250	880-1000	15-40	135-360
86-95	190-210	100-110	400-440	225-260	900-1040	15-40	135-360
over 95	over 210	100-115	400-460	230-260	920-1040	20-45	180-405

COMPETITIVE FEMALE BODYBUILDER TRAINING 2 HOURS, 6 TIMES A WEEK, FOR QUICK FAT LOSS AND MUSCLE GAIN

MINIMUM REQUIRED DAILY INTAKE OF PROTEIN, CARBOHYDRATES, AND FAT

Body Weight		Protein		Carbohydrates		Fat	
KILOGRAMS	POUNDS	GRAMS	CALORIES	GRAMS	CALORIES	GRAMS	CALORIES
40-45	90-100	70-80	280-320	60-80	240-320	10-15	90-225
45-55	100-120	70-85	280-340	70-90	280-360	10-25	90-225
55-68	120-150	80-100	320-400	80-110	320-440	10-25	90-225
68-77	150-170	90-110	360-440	90-120	360-480	10-30	90-270
77-86	170-190	100-120	400-480	100-140	400-560	10-30	90-270
86-95	190-210	105-120	420-480	110-150	440-600	10-30	90-270
over 95	over 210	110-120	440-480	100-160	400-640	10-30	90-270

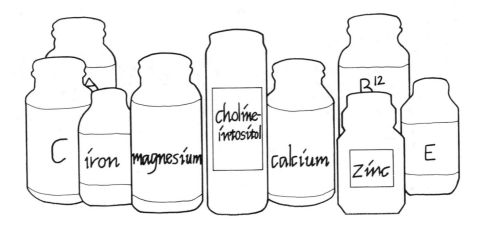

4

SUPPLEMENTS
VITAMINS AND MINERALS

When it comes to taking vitamins and minerals, the average person is directed by tables of Recommended Daily Allowances (RDAs) established by the Food and Nutrition Board Research Council. These tables, originally designed as guidelines for labeling products, are ideal for individuals not involved in sports or other activities that place great demands on body systems. For this reason, many of the supplements suggested for bodybuilders show an increase in daily allowances otherwise recommended. Some are only slightly higher than established by the council; others are much higher, according to the intensity of individual training programs. For example, a bodybuilder aiming only for an improved physical appearance and increased strength would take 1,000 mg of calcium per day. A professional, having his eye fixed on entering national or international competition would raise his daily intake to 3,000 mg of calcium.

Essentially, vitamins are organic substances, a small amount of which must be included in the daily diet to sustain life. When they are lacking, a deficiency disease develops. Vitamins in themselves are not a source of energy but act in conjunction with enzyme systems to free energy from carbohydrates, fats, and protein. Vitamins must come from food or supplements because our bodies are unable to manufacture them. Never consider vitamins a substitute for food. Instead, concentrate on their supportive role in the maintenance of all body systems.

Vitamins are designated as either fat-soluble (dissolving in fat and oil) or water-soluble (dissolving in water). Vitamins A, D, E, and K, which are fat-soluble, can be stored in the body. Water-soluble vitamins, including the B-complex group and vitamin C, cannot be stored in appreciable amounts save for a few exceptions. Being components of essential enzyme systems, they must be supplied daily. Some bodybuilders may not realize they are deficient in some nutrient until they experience a surge of energy from taking a particular vitamin or mineral supplement. In this case it should be increased within a reasonable limit above the amount suggested.

Some vitamins and minerals may cause allergic reactions, evidenced by nausea, diarrhea, or other adverse effects as described under the heading for each supplement on the following pages. In such instances I suggest trying two or three brands of the same vitamin or mineral. If the problem persists, discontinue its use for a month before attempting to take it again. Many people cannot tolerate some of the B-complex vitamins due to their yeast content. Fortunately, some manufacturers are now producing a hypoallergenic line that is yeast-free.

Minerals, unlike vitamins, do serve as part of the body structure in a manner similar to proteins; however, they are found mainly in bone rather than muscle tissue. Minerals must also be supplied by the intake of food and supplements. Our body systems require a number of different types to maintain health. For bodybuilders, some minerals, like calcium, are needed in greater amounts than others, such as copper, chromium, and zinc. Women usually need more iron than men because they utilize a little extra when training to build additional blood cells and for the monthly cycle of menstruation. Mainly, minerals are far less vulnerable than vitamins to destruction in food processing or storage, so a discussion of their properties in this area is limited to a few exceptions.

If it were possible to eat a large variety of good food throughout the year, we could avoid the expense of supplementing our diet with vitamins and minerals. Unfortunately, most of us cannot buy perfect food. Fruits and vegetables promise greater profits to growers if they are picked green to prevent bruising and wilting during the process of being packed and shipped to the local supermarket. Shoppers suffer the loss of vitamins and minerals that are unable to form unless produce has ripened to maturity. Also, food preservatives can destroy as much as 80 percent of the nutrients contained in many foods, despite their careful packaging in a sanitary environment.

Other problems revolve around eating only food we like on a consistent basis rather than aiming for variety. Many individuals utilize nutrients at a greater rate than others due to job stress or the expectations of society, family, and friends. Bodybuilders who enter competitive events carry an extra burden of stress because of hard training and the tension that accompanies the contest. Being bodybuilders, we need to supplement our dietary intake with vitamins and minerals, while the average person may safely exclude them. After all, most people only jog a few miles, eat, and then relax in front of a television set.

My own experiences with food in relation to supplements has brought several interesting points into focus. When my intake of meat and eggs is high I don't feel the need to take any vitamins in the B-complex group; however, I find it necessary to increase my intake of minerals. On the other hand, a diet high in fish and eggs increases my need for vitamins and decreases the necessity for minerals. This is easily explained by the fact that training utilizes a high percentage of minerals such as calcium, magnesium, zinc, sodium, and phosphorus. Fish supplies these needs because it contains a rich store of minerals. On the contrary, meat and liver are low in minerals but high in the B-complex vitamins.

When eating a great deal of fish, I found it possible to decrease my intake of mineral supplements because I suffered far less from cramps. The minerals in fish also prevented softening of my tooth enamel, caused by eating a lot of pineapple. On several occasions I experimented with diets, including a high intake of meat and pineapple. This immediately caused problems with softened tooth enamel until my diet was supplemented with additional calcium. These are a few examples of the lessons learned from paying careful attention to the unique needs of my own body. In general, however, it is my opinion that the three most essential supplements for bodybuilders are vitamin B_6 to build muscle tissue, choline to emulsify fat and gain definition, and calcium to become strong and to prevent cramps.

On the following pages I discuss all the vitamins and minerals fully, together with reasons for taking them. In this way you can avoid chemically unbalancing your body with megadoses recommended by a friend or gym instructor who is badly informed on the subject of nutrients. A full awareness of the supplements actually needed, when coupled with an understanding of their role in muscle growth, definition, and body maintenance, will save you money by eliminating the expense of buying unnecessary vitamins and minerals.

HYDROCHLORIC ACID AND ENZYMES

Under normal conditions, enzyme supplements are not necessary since they are found in a number of food items, such as papaya and pineapple. Even wine contains many enzymes needed to aid the digestive process. Hydrochloric acid is not found in food, however, but must be produced by the body or taken in supplemental form. When your intake of protein is increased, you must also take care to increase proportionally your intake of HCl. As a rule of thumb, every additional 20 grams of protein above amounts listed on the food charts requires 100 additional mg of HCl. It can be purchased in combination with enzymes or simply in the form of hydrochloric acid. Some bodybuilders find that HCl alone suffices; others need the combination of both supplements.

In conclusion, I would like to point out that bodybuilders' muscles are kept flexible due to the attention paid to taking vitamins and minerals. Calcium, for instance, not only maintains muscle flexibility but also enhances the proper balance of phosphorus in the body systems that is responsible for a chemical harmony of nutrients. Until today little attention was paid to the fact that bodybuilders' muscles are hard when flexed but soft and pliable when relaxed. Compare this interesting phenomenon with the physical condition of American runners, whose muscles are hard and spastic, whether flexed or relaxed. Runners have this problem for several reasons: (1) lack of muscle flexibility; (2) buildup of lactic acid from marathon running; and (3) the necessity to keep running after the body has depleted its supply of calcium.

Many people who visit my chiropractic office ask, "How can you possibly adjust bodybuilders when they are so muscular?"

"They are the easiest patients to adjust," I answer, much to their surprise. When I ask a bodybuilder to relax—an important condition for a proper adjustment—they are capable of immediately letting go because their muscles have remained flexible rather than taut. On the other hand, marathon runners who come for an adjustment have hard, spastic muscle. When I ask them to relax, their muscles remain unchanged. My suggestion to marathon runners preparing to run 25 kilometers would include taking a lot of calcium before the event and even during the run—after going about 10 kilometers. Immediately afterward they should take calcium again and stretch a great deal to maintain muscle flexibility.

BEST TIME TO TAKE SUPPLEMENTS

"When should I take my vitamin and mineral supplements?" is a question often asked by young bodybuilders and others coming to my clinic for training programs. As a rule of thumb, I recommend taking them before, during, or directly after meals to avoid the digestive upset experienced by some individuals who take them on an empty stomach. In so doing, an additional benefit is gained: the nutrients in the supplements integrate with those in food, making for a faster rate of absorption into the bloodstream.

All the supplements may be taken at one time, but their value is increased when the daily intake is divided into equal portions that accompany separate meals. For instance, instead of taking three vitamin B_{12} capsules each morning, take the first with breakfast, the second with lunch, and the third with dinner. This method is particularly effective when applied to the water-soluble vitamins that comprise the B-complex group. Since the body has little capacity to store them, only the amount needed is absorbed by the body; the remainder is excreted in the urine within a few hours. If you take them all in the morning and work out late in the afternoon, only an insignificant amount remains for use in your body systems. The fat-soluble vitamins (A, D, E, K) may all be taken at once because a certain amount is stored in the liver and other body organs.

Athletes and others in hard training lose some nutrients faster than others. Profuse sweating causes a loss of vitamin C, which should be replaced by taking a portion of the suggested amount soon after training.

SELECTING SUPPLEMENTS

The market for dietary supplements is highly competitive, making it difficult sometimes to choose the best buy for your hard-earned money. I have, therefore, set forth some guidelines to help in your selection.

1. Choose supplements in the form of multivitamins and minerals found together in one bottle. Select those for which the indicated potency most closely matches dosages suggested on the charts. Because most supplements are intended for the average person rather than bodybuilders, the amounts shown on labels will not always correspond to those indicated on the charts. For this reason, it will be necessary to purchase others in addition to the multivitamins and minerals, such as vitamin B_6, choline and inositol (usually found together), calcium, and enzymes.

2. Check expiration dates stamped on labels, choosing only those dated two or more years ahead of the purchase date, although salespeople may tell you that supplements have a shelf life of three years. Most of them are not trying to mislead you but sincerely believe this is true. I am of the opinion that supplements cannot maintain their full potency for three years. So, if you are buying supplements in 1984, do not select any with expiration dates in 1985—meaning they were produced in 1982. Instead, choose those marked 1986 or 1987 because their nutritional value is more stable.

3. Always buy high-potency products. This significantly reduces the amount of coating or binder used in making tablets and capsules.

4. Carefully read all labels, selecting only those supplements identified as free from additives such as artificial color, preservatives, and sugar. When this is not specified on the label, additives were probably used to give the supplements eye appeal or to make them taste better.

5. To assure more complete assimilation of minerals by the body systems, try to get chelated minerals, which are 10 times more digestible than nonchelated.

Note: Many of the symptoms discussed for vitamin and mineral deficiencies can occur only when the daily intake of any particular nutrient falls below the minimum daily requirement over a long period of time. These nonspecific symptoms alone are not proof of

Men: Suggested Daily Intake

	Average	Noncompetitive	Competitive
VITAMINS			
Vitamin A	20,000 IU	30,000 IU	50,000 IU
Vitamin B_1 (thiamine)	100 mg	150 mg	150 mg
Vitamin B_2 (riboflavin)	100 mg	150 mg	150 mg
Vitamin B_6	200 mg	350 mg	500 mg
Vitamin B_{12}	300 mg	300 mg	500 mg
Biotin	100 mcg	100 mcg	100 mcg
Choline	200 mg	500 mg	2,000 mg
Folic acid	300 mcg	400 mcg	400 mcg
Inositol	200 mg	500 mg	2,000 mg
Niacin (niacinamide)	100 mg	150 mg	200 mg
Pantothenic acid	100 mg	300 mg	500 mg
Para-aminobenzoic acid (PABA)	75 mg	100 mg	200 mg
Vitamin C (ascorbic acid)	1,000 mg	2,000 mg	3-4,000 mg
Vitamin D	300 IU	400 IU	400 IU
Vitamin E	1,000 IU	1,000 IU	1,500 IU
MINERALS			
Calcium	1,000 mg	2,000 mg	3,000 mg
Chromium	700 mcg	750 mcg	750 mcg
Copper	2 mg	2 mg	2 mg
Iodine	20 mg	20 mg	20 mg
Iron	20 mg	20 mg	20 mg
Magnesium	500 mg	1,000 mg	1,500 mg
Manganese	20 mg	40 mg	80 mg
Phosphorus	50 mg	50 mg	50 mg
Potassium	200 mg	500 mg	600-1,000 mg
Selenium	100 mcg	100 mcg	100 mcg
ENZYMES HYDROCHLORIC ACID			
Amylase	25 mg	50 mg	50 mg
Beatine HCl	100 mg	200 mg	200 mg
Bromelain	50 mg	50 mg	50 mg
Lipase	25 mg	50 mg	50 mg
Ox bile	30 mg	30 mg	30 mg
Pancreas substance	100 mg	200 mg	250 mg
Papain	50 mg	100 mg	150 mg
Pepsin	50 mg	100 mg	100 mg
Protease	100 mg	150 mg	300 mg

Women: Suggested Daily Intake

	Average	Noncompetitive	Competitive
VITAMINS			
Vitamin A	20,000 IU	30,000 IU	50,000 IU
Vitamin B$_1$ (thiamine)	100 mg	150 mg	150 mg
Vitamin B$_2$ (riboflavin)	100 mg	150 mg	150 mg
Vitamin B$_6$	250 mg	300 mg	500 mg
Vitamin B$_{12}$	300 mcg	300 mcg	500 mcg
Biotin	100 mcg	100 mcg	100 mcg
Choline	1,000 mg	1,500 mg	2,000 mg
Folic acid	300 mcg	400 mcg	400 mcg
Inositol	1,000 mg	1,500 mg	2,000 mg
Niacin (niacinamide)	100 mg	150 mg	200 mg
Pantothenic acid	100 mg	300 mg	500 mg
Para-aminobenzoic acid (PABA)	75 mg	100 mg	200 mg
Vitamin C (ascorbic acid)	1,000 mg	2,000 mg	3-4,000 mg
Vitamin D	300 IU	400 IU	400 IU
Vitamin E	1,000 IU	1,000 IU	1,500 IU
MINERALS			
Calcium	1,000 mg	2,000 mg	3,000 mg
Chromium	700 mcg	750 mcg	750 mcg
Copper	2 mg	2 mg	2 mg
Iodine	20 mg	20 mg	20 mg
Iron	20 mg	30 mg	40 mg
Magnesium	500 mg	1,000 mg	1,500 mg
Manganese	20 mg	40 mg	80 mg
Phosphorus	50 mg	50 mg	50 mg
Potassium	200 mg	500 mg	600-1,000 mg
Selenium	100 mcg	100 mcg	100 mcg
Zinc	50 mg	50 mg	100 mg
ENZYMES HYDROCHLORIC ACID			
Amylase	25 mg	50 mg	50 mg
Beatine HCl	100 mg	200 mg	300 mg
Bromelain	50 mg	50 mg	50 mg
Lipase	25 mg	50 mg	50 mg
Ox bile	30 mg	30 mg	30 mg
Pancreas substance	100 mg	200 mg	250 mg
Papain	50 mg	100 mg	150 mg
Pepsin	50 mg	100 mg	100 mg
Protease	100 mg	150 mg	300 mg

nutritional deficiencies but may be caused by any of a great number of conditions or may have functional causes. If the symptoms persist, they may indicate a condition other than a vitamin or mineral deficiency. When any of the symptoms do persist it would be wise to consult your doctor.

VITAMINS

VITAMIN A

Vitamin A, discovered in 1913, was the first fat-soluble vitamin to be recognized. It occurs in two forms: provitamin A or carotene (found in foods of animal and plant origin) and preformed vitamin A or retinol (found only in foods of animal origin). Most of our dietary supply comes from carotene, so called because it was first prepared from carrots, although a high concentration is also found in deep yellow fruits and vegetables and dark green vegetables. It should be understood that carotene is not the vitamin itself, but a provitamin, meaning it is converted in the intestinal walls during the process of digestion as well as in the liver to produce the true vitamin A.

Retinol, on the other hand, is immediately ready to work in the body since it comes from animals who have already transformed carotene from plant sources into the true vitamin A. Being preformed, retinol is absorbed by the body almost twice as fast as carotene from vegetables.

Bodybuilders need vitamin A to maintain firm and healthy skin tone so they avoid looking worn and wrinkled onstage. Also, their need to concentrate on definition demands a low percentage of body fat, which can make them more susceptible to infection. To compensate for this possibility, those in hard training for several months before a contest can increase their intake of Vitamin A to 50,000 units, while 10,000 are sufficient for the average bodybuilder.

Functions The most well-known function of vitamin A is the prevention of night blindness, the inability of the eyes to adjust to changes in light intensity. Vitamin A also maintains the health of tissues lining every passage opening to the exterior of the body. By protecting the mucous membranes of the nose, throat, mouth, and lungs, it combats irritation caused by air pollutants and reduces susceptibility to infection. In a similar way, the soft tissues and linings of the bladder, kidneys, and digestive tract are protected. While vitamin A does not combat existing infections, a deficiency of the vitamin weakens this protective power of the mucous membranes and sets up conditions allowing infections to occur more easily.

Many people respond better to vitamin A than to C when trying to ward off a cold, particularly if they take A in the form of unconcentrated fish liver oil. Additional dosages should be taken in the beginning stages of a cold instead of waiting until it hits full force. Used externally, vitamin A has proved effective in the treatment of skin disorders such as acne and boils. For these conditions, the high dosage usually required must be prescribed by a doctor. Normal intake is needed for bone growth, reproduction, and healthy skin, hair, teeth, and gums.

Deficiency symptoms   When internal disorders interfere with the absorption and storage of vitamin A, deficiencies can occur. Certain diabetics, for instance, convert only 25 percent of the carotene from plant sources into the vitamin; therefore, they should obtain the recommended allowance from animal sources and supplements.

One of the first symptoms of a deficiency is night blindness. Correctly diagnosed, however, it can be cured in less than an hour by an injection of vitamin A. Other symptoms are dry, scaly skin; increased susceptibility to respiratory infections; and the formation of kidney and bladder stones. Prolonged deficiency leads to the rapid loss of vitamin C.

Destroys vitamin or limits absorption   Alcohol, caffeine, charcoal, cortisone, excessive iron, mineral oil, and vitamin D deficiency destroy vitamin A.

Because strenuous physical activity interferes with absorption, supplements should be taken four hours before or after working out.

Toxicity   Symptoms of the prolonged, excessive intake of vitamin A include extreme irritability, loss of appetite, bone pain, blurred vision, drowsiness, diarrhea, and nausea. When toxicity is diagnosed and the vitamin is withdrawn, symptoms usually disappear within a few days. Generally, toxicity occurs only when someone takes over 100,000 IU of straight vitamin A for several months. The most famous cases of overdosing took place in the Arctic Circle, where some explorers ate over a pound of polar bear liver every day, containing about *9,000,000* IU of vitamin A. Since I have yet to see polar bear liver stocked in any market, toxicity from that source is unlikely.

Storage   Light and air destroy this vitamin, so store animal fat, vegetables, and ripe fruit in the refrigerator. Carrots should be used within two weeks, leafy vegetables and broccoli within three to five days. Fish liver oil should be kept in a dark bottle and stored in a cool place.

Processing effects   Vitamin loss during cooking averages 15–20 percent for green vegetables and 30–35 percent for those with yellow coloring. Steaming retains the highest percentage of vitamins, while boiling causes the greatest loss. Charbroiling meat and fish is destructive to vitamin A.

Best sources   Carrots, dandelion greens, fish liver oil, and liver.

Good sources

Animal   Butter, cheese, crab, cream, egg yolk, halibut, kidney, oysters, salmon, swordfish, and whole milk.

Fruit   Apricots, cantaloupe, mangoes, papayas, and peaches.

Grains, nuts, seeds   Yellow cornmeal.

Vegetables   Beet tops, broccoli, cabbage leaves (green), collards, escarole, kale, mustard greens, parsley (raw), pumpkins, spinach, Swiss chard, sweet potatoes, turnip greens, and yellow winter squash.

Selection   Reject vegetables that look wilted and fruit that is very soft or shriveled. The content of carotene is highest in plant foods with dark green or deep yellow coloring. In other words, spinach, beet greens, and dandelion greens are rich sources of provitamin A, while lettuce contains an insignificant amount. Buy fruits and vegetables such as apricots, cantaloupe, carrots, and winter squash with a deep yellow color, indicating a high concentration of the provitamin. Because this color is so intense, it is used by the food industry as a coloring agent under the name of *beta carotene*. Select fresh apricots and peaches because dried fruit yields 50 percent less of the vitamin.

B-COMPLEX VITAMINS

When vitamin B was discovered it seemed to be a single

substance like vitamin A; however, scientists eventually found that it contains two separate factors, so they called one *vitamin B₁* or *thiamine* and the other *vitamin B₂* or *riboflavin.* Additional research showed that riboflavin also could be broken down, and further discoveries were made until a number of different substances were defined as making up the B-complex group, including vitamin B$_1$ (thiamine), vitamin B$_2$ (riboflavin), vitamin B$_6$, vitamin B$_{12}$, biotin, choline, folic acid, and niacin. Because most are found together in the same foods, a deficiency in one usually indicates a deficiency in several. It's useful to think of the B-complex vitamins as a team that must be kept together to achieve results. If an additional dosage of one, such as vitamin B$_6$, is required, it should be taken along with the others.

All the B-complex vitamins are water-soluble and have certain characteristics in common. Only a small amount can be stored in the body; therefore, they must be included in your diet every day. Acting as coenzymes, they convert carbohydrates into the glucose needed for energy and help to break down the protein and fats in food. They are considered one of the chief factors in maintaining a healthy nervous system, with the need for them increasing under physical and mental stress. Although many of their functions are the same, each member of this vitamin team performs a specific job within the body that will not allow one to replace the other any more than a running back can replace a lineman.

VITAMIN B$_1$ (THIAMINE)

Most often referred to as thiamine, vitamin B$_1$ was first used to cure beriberi, a disease of the nervous system primarily affecting people in rice-eating countries such as China. Beriberi simply means "I cannot" because those suffering from the disease had a deadening sensation in their muscles, preventing them from moving around without great effort. This was due to the lack of thiamine in their diet of polished rice. In milling, the husk of the grain containing the vitamin was removed to give the rice an appealing white color and a finer texture. To some extent, the same process is followed in manufacturing the packages of rice, white flour, and cereals stacked on shelves in local supermarkets. For this reason, I recommend including brown rice in many of the diets prescribed in this book. Keep in mind that thiamine should be included in the diet every day since the body has less capacity to store this water-soluble vitamin than any other and, although small amounts are found in many different foods, it is abundant in very few.

Functions   For bodybuilders, one of the most important functions of thiamine is promoting the breakdown of carbohydrates into the glucose needed to produce energy. In other words, if the intake of thiamine is low, carbohydrates may turn into body fat, but when an adequate amount is included in the daily diet, carbohydrates are broken down and converted into energy. This helps maintain a healthy nervous system, giving thiamine the reputation of being a morale-lifting vitamin.

Studies have showed that the need for it increases when people are under physical or emotional stress. Also, acting as a coenzyme, it manufactures hydrochloric acid to aid digestion and helps keep muscles of the digestive tract in good tone. It is necessary to promote growth and prevents an influx of pyruvic acid in the blood that might otherwise cause an oxygen deficiency. Some people have benefited from its use in the treatment of herpes.

Deficiency symptoms   A moderate deficiency will cause muscular weakness, a sensation of numbness in the legs, and painful calf muscles. This may be accompanied by feelings of being tired, moody, and nervous. Lack of ambition or apathy can be caused by a thiamine deficiency.

Destroys vitamin or limits absorption   Large amounts of tea; raw seafood, particularly clams, shrimp, and herring, which contain enzymes causing thiamine molecules to split in two and thus deactivate them; and excessive sugar and alcohol will destroy or limit absorption of vitamin B_1.

Toxicity   None.

Storage   Because thiamine is not destroyed by air, no significant loss of the vitamin occurs when grain foods are kept at room temperature.

Processing effects   From 15 to 25 percent of thiamine content is lost when baking bread, preparing hot cereal, and steaming vegetables. The loss almost doubles with cooked meat. When bread is toasted, a considerable loss of thiamine can occur due to the high, dry heat.

Best sources   Brewer's yeast, cornflakes (fortified), red-skinned peanuts, lean pork, torula yeast.

Good sources

Animal   Canadian bacon, kidneys, liver.

Fruit   A small amount is found in most fruits.

Grains, nuts, seeds   Alfalfa seeds, almonds, Brazil nuts, bread (enriched), chestnuts, cornmeal (enriched), pecans, pine nuts, rice bran, rice polishings, safflower seeds, sunflower seeds, sesame seeds, soybean flour, walnuts, wheat bran, wheat flour, wheat germ, whole barley, whole cereals, and whole wheat.

Vegetables   A small amount is found in most vegetables.

Selection   Buy brown rice rather than white. If whole grain products are not available in your area, read package labels and select only those that have been enriched with the B-complex vitamins, including thiamine.

Do not discard the red skins of peanuts; they are high in the B vitamins and an excellent source of niacin and riboflavin.

VITAMIN B$_2$ (RIBOFLAVIN)

Riboflavin, or vitamin B$_2$, has the distinction of being the only vitamin found in significant amounts in beer. A little over one quart almost meets the daily requirements. In general, however, a little is found in most foods of plant and animal origin, but B$_2$ is missing entirely from pure sugar and fats. Being a water-soluble vitamin, it is not stored in the body, so it should be included in the daily diet. Riboflavin, like other members of the B-complex group, is most active working in a partnership with other B vitamins to form enzymes and coenzymes. Although it is found naturally in foods containing other B vitamins, the amount is usually so small that obtaining a sufficient supply is difficult without supplementing the average daily diet. Most deficiencies occur in poor countries lacking a sufficient supply of eggs, milk, and meat. If your diet restricts the use of dairy products or red meat, your daily intake of riboflavin should be increased.

Functions   Bodybuilders should keep in mind that riboflavin is one of the vitamins that help release energy from amino acids, fatty acids, and carbohydrates while they are undergoing the process of metabolism. This energy is released gradually to every cell in the body system, being necessary for cell respiration and producing enzymes to maintain good vision and healthy skin, nails, and hair. It is necessary for activating vitamin B$_6$ and forming niacin from the amino acid tryptophan. Some authorities claim large doses will reduce the craving for cake, candy, and other sugar-loaded foods.

Deficiency symptoms   In America severe deficiencies seldom occur except among the aged and individuals on diets lacking both amimal protein and green, leafy vegetables. Also, a deficiency in riboflavin usually indicates other B-complex vitamins may be lacking in the diet. Feeling tired without good reason is one of the major symptoms. If fatigue accompanies or follows particularly stressful situations, you may be lacking riboflavin in addition to the other B vitamins. At times, a deficiency will cause your eyes to become sensitive to light, and they may also get bloodshot. Small cuts or wounds will not heal easily, and cracks may develop at the corners of the mouth if you are deficient in this vitamin.

Destroys vitamin or limits absorption   Alcohol, estrogen, and sulfa drugs destroy riboflavin. Sodium bicarbonate used in cooking vegetables is destructive to riboflavin. Because B_2 is easily destroyed by light, milk should be kept in cartons and all supplements in dark bottles.

Toxicity   None.

Storage   Over 50 percent of the riboflavin content of foods is lost when exposed to light for more than two hours. Those who lament days gone by when milk was delivered in clear glass bottles to the back doorstep should be aware that more than half the riboflavin content was lost as bottles stood outside basking in the early morning sunshine. Basically, however, this is one of the most stable vitamins, not affected by the fluctuating room temperatures found in most kitchens. So, cereals and other grain products can be stored safely in closed boxes on the kitchen shelves. As mentioned above, all vitamin supplements should be kept in dark bottles.

Processing effects   Being one of the heat-stable vitamins, very little riboflavin is lost during the process of cooking unless sodium bicarbonate is added to maintain the green color of vegetables. Also, riboflavin is barely water-soluble, so little is lost in any process involving large amounts of water.

Best sources   Beer, brewer's yeast, heart, kidneys, liver.

Good sources

Animal   Bacon, beef, cheese, chicken (dark meat), eggs, lamb, milk, mackerel, mutton, pork, sardines.

Fruit Avocados, grapefruit, mangoes, peaches, prunes, pears.

Grains, nuts, seeds Almonds, cornflakes (enriched), cornmeal (enriched), pecans, peanuts, rice polishings, rye flour, soybean flour, wheat flour (enriched), wheat bran, wheat germ, white bread (enriched).

Vegetables Beet greens, broccoli, collards, dandelion greens, endive, escarole, lettuce (green), kale, mustard greens, mushrooms (raw), turnip greens.

Selection Read the labels on grain products, selecting those that have been enriched with riboflavin. Try to purchase organ meats from animals not injected with hormones.

VITAMIN B₆ (PYRIDOXINE)

Considering the entire family of B-complex vitamins, none is more important to bodybuilders than B_6 as it plays an essential role in the metabolism of proteins and the assimilation of amino acids. To a lesser extent, it is also involved in the metabolism of carbohydrates and fats.

The most dramatic example of the benefits derived from taking this vitamin occurred in 1981 when I was training for the Mr. Olympia contest. It was then that I discovered that vitamin B_6 was highly important to the assimilation of amino acids. Until this time I was conservative in my use of vitamins, taking them only in small amounts, but when I came to understand the role played by B_6 in breaking down amino acids for building muscle tissue, I decided to take 500 mg daily for eight weeks. At the end of this time I noticed a change in my muscle growth that I had never experienced before. For this reason, I became a firm believer in vitamin B_6 when it comes to bodybuilding.

In general, I recommend 250–500 mg of this vitamin to those who train hard and want to increase muscle tissue. However, the daily intake is dependent on the amount of protein included in your diet as follows:

PROTEIN	VITAMIN B₆
100 g	250 mg
125 g	500 mg
150 g	750 mg
175 g	1,000 mg

By adjusting your intake of vitamin B_6 according to the amount of protein consumed, you can proportion your body as I did in winning the Mr. Olympia competition in 1981.

Functions   Some bodybuilders take diuretics to reduce the amount of water held in their muscle tissues. I find that vitamin B_6 serves as a natural diuretic, aiding in the prevention of water buildup in body tissues without damaging side effects. Many diuretic pills cause chemical imbalances in the body systems and can cause kidney problems, but vitamin B_6 will be as effective as any diuretic without causing health problems.

Also important to bodybuilders is the function of converting glycogen to the glucose needed for energy. At the same time, it assists in the functioning of the central nervous system and, like the other B-complex vitamins, aids in the treatment of stress. By helping to maintain a balance of sodium and potassium, it regulates the body fluids, thereby promoting normal functioning of the muscle and skeletal systems. Without it, vitamin B_{12} could not be absorbed and assimilated properly and the production of hydrochloric acid and magnesium would be inhibited. Like riboflavin, it helps in the conversion of tryptophan, one of the essential amino acids.

Bear in mind that a daily supply is needed along with other B-complex vitamins. If taken alone it can cause imbalance or deficiency in other B vitamins. Although it facilitates the release of glycogen for energy from the muscles and liver, it is not stored in the liver and is excreted from the body within eight hours after taking it.

Deficiency symptoms   Low blood sugar and low glucose tolerance are two deficiencies that can be measured in tests given by your doctor. Deficiencies may also manifest themselves as muscular weakness, nervousness, depression, and sores on the skin, particularly at the nose tip. Drastic reducing diets and fasting can severely deplete the body's supply if sufficient supplements are not taken. And be aware that many B-complex tablets contain very little B_6 because it is one of the more expensive vitamins. Some people believe a deficiency in vitamin B_6 prevents them from remembering their dreams.

Destroys vitamin or limits absorption   Alcohol, caffeine, birth control pills, radiation, canning, estrogen, and certain food-processing techniques can destroy or limit B_6 absorption.

Toxicity This vitamin is relatively nontoxic although injections of large doses can cause sleepiness in some people and night restlessness in others. An imbalance or deficiency in other B vitamins can occur if too much B_6 is taken alone.

Storage Since most losses of this vitamin occur in canning or freezing, no additional damage is done by storing products containing this vitamin.

Processing effects Over 80 percent of the vitamin B_6 content of wheat is lost during the milling of white flour, and it is not included in the list of vitamins used to enrich most white bread. Cooking beef, fruits, and vegetables at home results in a vitamin loss of approximately 50 percent, with the highest loss in beef occurring when it is fried at high temperatures.

Best sources Brewer's yeast, rice bran, rice polishings, sunflower seeds, torula yeast, wheat bran, wheat germ.

Good sources

Animal Beef kidneys, beef liver, beef round, chicken, chicken giblets, chicken liver, halibut, mackerel, pork loin, salmon, tuna.

Fruit Avocados, bananas.

Grains, nuts, seeds Brown rice, cereal (whole wheat), peanuts (roasted), soybean flour, walnuts, whole wheat flour.

Vegetables Not a good source.

Selection Avoid purchasing canned or frozen products since a considerable loss of vitamin B_6 occurs during the manufacturing process. For this reason, fresh tuna, salmon, and mackerel are far better nutritionally and have the advantage of lacking preservatives such as salt and oil. If you live in areas where fresh tuna is not available, but only water-packed tuna without added salt.

VITAMIN B_{12} (COBALAMIN)

Although many bodybuilders believe in getting vitamin B_{12} shots, I find their effectiveness limited. When the vitamin is injected directly into the body, going into the bloodstream, it lasts only about four hours. Therefore, to be as effective as claimed, it would be necessary to get a vitamin B_{12} shot every four hours. I don't believe anyone is willing to do this. On the other hand, when the vitamin is taken in tablet form, it remains in the body for a much longer period of time. For example, its absorption in the small intestine alone takes about three hours, while only seconds are required for the absorption of the other B vitamins. Certainly, it is a good idea to have an adequate amount of vitamin B_{12}, but as a bodybuilder who wants to gain the most benefit from supplements, you would be far better off increasing your intake of vitamin B_6.

I realize that many bodybuilders believe vitamin B_{12} will work miracles that are perhaps better realized through hard training and a carefully controlled diet. Nevertheless, vitamin B_{12} holds a respected position in some bodybuilding circles, which leads me to believe that some of its actual benefits are psychological rather than physiological. Fortunately, through my training as a chiropractor and nutritionist, I learned to judge vitamins according to their regulatory effect on body functions instead of on their popular appeal.

Functions   The coenzymes found in vitamin B_{12} are essential to normal maturation of red blood cells. Without these coenzymes, large, unhealthy cells would enter the bloodstream, resulting in anemia, especially in the cells of the bone marrow. Like other B-complex vitamins, B_{12} is vital to maintaining a healthy nervous system since it is necessary for the synthesis of lipoproteins basic to the structure of nervous tissue. In addition, it is required for the metabolism of protein, fats, and carbohydrates.

Deficiency symptoms   Many pure vegetarians who consume no animal foods, including milk, eggs, and cheese, suffer a deficiency in this vitamin. Often it is difficult to detect because their diets are usually low in vitamin B_1 and high in folic acid, a combination that hides a deficiency in B_{12}. Because a certain amount of this vitamin is stored in the liver, kidneys, muscles, lungs, and spleen, it sometimes takes as long as five years to discover the deficiency. It is only when these natural sources in the body have been depleted that the problem is diagnosed.

Symptoms of a deficiency begin with changes in the nervous system manifested by diminished reflexes, weakness in the arms and legs, poor appetite, and nervousness.

Destroys vitamin or limits absorption   Most laxatives, tobacco, alcohol, caffeine, estrogen, and sleeping pills taken over extended periods of time destroy the vitamin or limit its absorption. It is also destroyed by light.

Storage   As mentioned above, light destroys vitamin B_{12}, so keep supplements stored in dark-colored bottles.

Processing effects   Ordinary home cooking causes a loss of about 30–35 percent of this vitamin. Meat should be broiled. Fish can either be steamed or broiled.

Best sources   Kidneys, liver, heart.

Good sources

Animal   Beef, bologna, catfish, clams, cod, crab, eggs, frankfurters, halibut, herring, lamb, liverwurst, mackerel, mozzarella, oysters, pork, salmon, sardines, sausage, Swiss cheese, tuna.

Fruit   Very small amounts are found in plant foods because they cannot manufacture vitamin B_{12}, although they do absorb trace amounts from the soil.

Grains, nuts, seeds   Same as for fruit.

Vegetables   Same as for fruit.

Selection   Although vitamin B_{12} is found in a number of canned, smoked, and highly salted foods, it is best obtained from fresh food sources.

VITAMIN B_{13} (OROTIC ACID)

To date, this is not readily available in the United States, although in Europe it has been found to be helpful in treating multiple sclerosis.

Many of its uses are still to be discovered, yet research shows it is one of the factors aiding in the metabolism of folic acid and vitamin B_{12}. In addition, it seems to play a role in the replacement and restoration of some cells. While it was found to stimulate the growth of laboratory animals, this is yet to be proved with humans.

Scientists are still working on the deficiency symptoms of orotic acid, but they have some evidence that a lack of it may cause cell degeneration, liver disorders, and premature aging.

Sources   Too little is known to establish other guidelines for its use; however, at present we know that food sources include sour or curdled milk, whey, and root vegetables like carrots, potatoes, and turnips.

VITAMIN B_{15} (PANGAMIC ACID)

Vitamin B_{15}, more often referred to as *pangamic acid,* has the dubious reputation of being responsible for the increased energy levels of Russian athletes. I have found that some manufacturers of American vitamins tend to credit the ingredients of any new product with having performed miracles in foreign countries, such as Russia and Switzerland. These claims are not based on fact but are created by copywriters struggling to earn a living just like everyone else. In truth, the superior performance of many Russian athletes is based on hard training, a carefully maintained diet, and discipline, established early in their lives with the guidance of highly experienced instructors.

Through the years, I have taken pangamic acid without experiencing any rise in my energy level; therefore, I cannot recommend it for bodybuilders. I can, however, offer the information that it has established a reputation in racing circles for enabling horses to run faster and tire less easily. I have yet to discover if the horses were American, Russian, or Swiss.

Although pangamic acid is classed as a vitamin, the Food and Drug Administration considers it a food additive since it is not organic in nature and no deficiency diseases have been documented from its lack in the diet. Pangamic acid was classed as a B vitamin when its sources were shown to be the same foods that are high in the other B-complex vitamins.

Deficiency symptoms   There is some evidence that a deficiency causes fatigue due to a lack of sufficient oxygen in the cellular system.

Toxicity   The only symptom of toxicity noted is nausea, yet the Food and Drug Administration is working to get this food supplement off the market.

Sources   The main sources are apricot kernels, brewer's yeast, brown rice, ginkgo seeds, liver, poppy seeds, pumpkin seeds, sesame seeds, sunflower seeds, and whole grain cereals.

VITAMIN B$_{17}$ (LAETRILE)

Laetrile is quite often classed with the B vitamins, although a controversy still exists as to whether or not it is a true vitamin or a vitaminlike substance. As yet, laetrile has no practical use for bodybuilders, but it is listed here since bodybuilders competing in foreign countries may hear it mentioned more often than in America.

Mainly, laetrile has built a reputation for having cancer-controlling properties and has been used for this purpose in Europe. In the United States laetrile has been rejected by the Food and Drug Administration on the ground that it may be poisonous because cyanide is found in the chemistry of the vitamin, obtained chiefly from the kernels of apricots. It is also found in the whole kernels of plums, nectarines, cherries, peaches, and apples.

Scientists in Russia and the United States agree that it does not cure cancer or treat it successfully even if caught early. While banned in the United States, it is used legally in many foreign countries, including Italy, Germany, and Mexico.

Toxicity   According to some nutritionists, 5–20 apricot kernels can be eaten in one day, but *never* all at the same time. In other words, no more than 1 gram should be taken at one time.

BIOTIN

Biotin is one of the water-soluble vitamins that make up the B-complex group.

Functions   Its most important function relating to bodybuilders is helping to release adenosine triphosphate (ATP), the main source of energy for muscular work. In addition, it is needed for the metabolism of carbohydrates, fats, and proteins.

Deficiency symptoms   Deficiencies are rare because biotin is found in a variety of foods from plants and animal sources. Only when a diet contains large amounts of raw egg white—as in eggnog—will problems occur. Avidin, a substance found in the whites, destroys biotin; however, when they are cooked, avidin becomes inactive. Any deficiency may cause dry scaly skin, loss of appetite, and muscle pains.

Toxicity   None.

Sources   The main sources are brewer's yeast, American cheese, chocolate, kidneys, liver, nuts, sardines, soybean flour, torula yeast, and whole grains.

CHOLINE

While a number of vitamins are essential to bodybuilding, B_6 is first in importance. Choline, another of the B vitamins, is second. As a bodybuilder, I have focused particular attention on vitamins playing a significant role in the *metabolism* of nutrients needed for building muscle and gaining definition. Choline is one of these.

Functions   The most essential function of choline is regulating the amount of fat accumulating in the liver. When you are in hard training and your intake of proteins is high, stress is placed on the liver, causing a slowdown in its activity. Even more wearing on this vital organ is the consumption of steroids. To rehabilitate the liver and facilitate the digestion of protein and enzymes, it is necessary to increase your intake of supplements containing choline. This will also minimize the excessive fat deposits that accumulate in the liver, since it is here that excess fat is first stored. Most likely, any bodybuilder who is smooth has excess deposits in both the liver and the surrounding area. When bodybuilders want to gain definition, it is necessary to rehabilitate the liver by working to rid themselves of the fat it has accumulated. Through my own experience I discovered that choline was highly efficient in performing this function. Before competing I raise my intake of choline from 1,000 to 4,000 mg per day. It has been found to function best when working with inositol, a key constituent of lecithin.

It also helps to emulsify cholesterol, preventing it from building up on artery walls or in the gallbladder. By working to keep the liver functioning properly, choline plays an important role in eliminating poisons and drugs from the body systems. It is noteworthy, too, that choline is one of the few substances that goes directly into the brain cells, producing chemicals that enhance memory.

Deficiency symptoms   High blood pressure, hardening of the arteries, and cirrhosis of the liver can result from a deficiency of choline for a long period of time. Dizziness and headaches are some of the early symptoms.

Destroys vitamin or limits absorption   Alcohol, caffeine, and sugar destroy or limit absorption of choline.

Toxicity   None, but some people may experience nausea or diarrhea.

Storage   In dried foods, including soybean flour, wheat germ, and rice bran, the content of choline remains stable for long periods of time. Eggs should be stored in their carton with the large ends up. Left at room temperature, an egg will age in one day approximately as much as in one week in the refrigerator.

Processing effects   Choline is one of the B vitamins that remains stable during any cooking process.

Best sources   Brewer's yeast, eggs, liver.

Good sources

Animal Beef heart, brains, buttermilk, kidneys, skimmed milk, sweetbreads, tongue.

Fruit Very low sources.

Grains, nuts, seeds Barley (whole grain), corn (whole grain), hominy, oats, rice (whole grain), rice bran, rice polishings, sorghum (whole grain), torula yeast, wheat bran, wheat flour.

Vegetables Blackstrap molasses, cabbage, navy beans, potatoes, soybeans, turnips.

Selection Eggs are one of the richest sources of choline, yet many people are afraid to eat them, believing the cholesterol they contain will lead to clogged arteries. Yet the cholesterol found in eggs is accompanied by lecithin, a waxy substance that not only nullifies the harmful substances in cholesterol but may also play an important role in lowering any risk of clogged arteries and heart attacks.

Larger eggs are usually a better buy per ounce, but smaller ones often have a better flavor. In testing eggs for freshness, prepare a solution of one pint of water mixed with 1½ tablespoons of table salt. If the egg sinks, it is fresh. If it floats, throw it away.

FOLIC ACID (FOLACIN)

This vitamin, first isolated from spinach, was originally called *folacin,* which stems from a Latin word meaning "leaf." Some of its richest sources are vegetables with large leaves, such as spinach and escarole.

Functions The inclusion of folic acid in the diet of bodybuilders is important for several reasons. In its role as one of the water-soluble B vitamins, it stimulates the production of hydrochloric acid, thereby helping in the breakdown of protein. Without a sufficient supply of folic acid, it would be necessary to increase your intake of hydrochloric acid supplements. It is also essential to the formation of a number of amino acids, including tyrosine and methionine. Working as a carrier for the iron-containing protein in hemoglobin, it is vital to the formation of red blood cells. The process of mitosis and cell reproduction throughout the body systems is also dependent on folic acid to synthesize DNA (deoxyribonucleic acid) and RNA (ribonucleic acid), elements vital to the nucleus of every cell.

Deficiency symptoms Digestive problems may be caused by a deficiency because folic acid works to break down proteins. Anemia and mental deterioration can also be caused by a lack of folic acid over an extended period of time.

Destroys vitamin or limits absorption   Chronic alcoholism, stress, tobacco, caffeine, boiling, and sunlight destroy or limit absorption of folic acid.

Toxicity   None known.

Storage   The green leafy vegetables should be stored in a crisper or plastic bag and used within two or three days. Do not wash asparagus before storing. Ideally, asparagus should be kept in a tall container, somewhat like flowers with their stems in about an inch of water. Lacking this ideal arrangement, store in a plastic bag or vegetable crisper. Room temperature for two days will destroy approximately 75 percent of their folic acid content.

Processing effects   Since boiling vegetables results in folic acid losses as high as 95 percent, they should be steamed until just tender. Canned vegetables lose over 75 percent of their folic acid content due to the volume of water and the high temperature used in preparing them.

Best sources   Brewer's yeast, kidneys, liver, spinach, torula yeast.

Good sources

Animal   Cheddar cheese, chicken giblets, egg yolks, fish (all types except cod and halibut).

Fruit   Avocados, bananas, oranges.

Grains, nuts, seeds   Almonds, Brazil nuts, cashews, peanuts, rye flour, walnuts, wheat germ, whole grain wheat products.

Vegetables   Asparagus, beets, broccoli, Brussels sprouts, cabbage, cauliflower, endive, garbanzo beans, green beans, lettuce, parsley, pumpkins, turnip greens, soybeans.

Selection   When buying spinach, escarole, and other vegetables with large leaves, pick those that have a good green color and crisp appearance. Reject any that have stains resembling rust or any wilted areas. Parsley should also appear crisp, without any yellow leaves. Asparagus is best when tips are closed and compact, and when purchased from markets that keep them standing upright in a small amount of water.

INOSITOL

Inositol is another of the water-soluble vitamins associated with the B complex group. Closely related to choline, it is found along with choline in the same supplements. It occurs in animal and plant tissues, and in humans it is stored chiefly in the brain and skeletal and heart muscles.

Functions   By promoting the production of lecithin, inositol helps in moving fats from the liver to the cells. By doing so it aids in the metabolism of fats and helps reduce cholesterol levels. In combination with choline it helps protect the heart by preventing any fatty hardening of the arteries. It is also helpful in brain cell nutrition. Many nutritionists claim it can prevent thinning hair and baldness, but most of their evidence came from research done in laboratories on rats, chicks, hamsters, and guinea pigs but not humans.

Deficiency symptoms   A deficiency may be evidenced by high blood cholesterol; however, this can be caused by other problems and should be diagnosed by a physician. Other symptoms are eczema and constipation.

Destroys vitamin or limits absorption   People who drink large amounts of coffee can deplete their body's store of this vitamin. Alcohol and sugar in excess will eventually do the same thing.

Toxicity   None known.

Storage   Like other members of the B-complex group, supplements should be stored in dark bottles.

Processing effects   Tests are still being conducted to determine inositol losses during cooking and storage of food products.

Best sources   Blackstrap molasses, bran, grapefruit, heart, lemons, limes, liver, oranges, wheat germ, yeast.

Good sources

Animal   Found in most cuts of meat and in milk.

Fruit   Found in all fruits.

Grains, nuts, seeds   Found in all nuts.

Vegetables   Found in all vegetables.

Selection   When buying blackstrap molasses, keep in mind that it is extracted from the same canes that yield sugar. Although blackstrap molasses is high in minerals, one tablespoon contains over 40 calories and 11 grams of carbohydrate.

NIACIN

Another of the B-complex vitamins is niacin. It, too, is water-soluble but is more stable than thiamine or riboflavin. Generally, it is found in two forms, nicotinic acid and niacinamide, with the latter preferred by certain people because it minimizes the flushing and itchy skin that sometimes accompanies taking the supplement.

Functions   Working with thiamine and riboflavin, it helps to release energy by burning starches and sugars. As a coenzyme, niacin is necessary for cell respiration. These two functions should be useful to bodybuilders when they are choosing vitamin supplements to increase energy levels. Research has shown that nicotinic acid reduces levels of cholesterol. The same is not true of niacinamide. By increasing circulation, niacin in either form promotes healthier-looking skin and alleviates disturbances in the intestinal tract.

Deficiency symptoms   At one time, the lack of niacin in the diet caused many people to die of pellagra, a skin disease. This condition was caused by diets without milk, meat, yeast, peas, beans, and other vegetables. Now there is little incidence of this disease except in Africa. Mild symptoms are irritability, depression, and anxiety. People with severe cases develop pellagra, diarrhea, and dysfunctions of the nervous system.

Destroys vitamin or limits absorption   Caffeine, alcohol, and antibiotics destroy or limit absorption.

Toxicity   Basically, this vitamin is nontoxic. People with sensitive skin, however, may get flushed or itchy skin from nicotinic acid. This is caused by the release of a histamine and is usually gone within 15–20 minutes. This effect can be minimized by taking the supplement directly before or after a meal.

Storage   Niacin withstands a reasonable amount of time in storage.

Processing effects   If only a little cooking water is used, niacin losses can be held at a minimum.

Best sources   Brewer's yeast, chicken breast, cornflakes (enriched), kidneys, liver, peanuts, rabbit, swordfish, torula yeast, turkey breast.

Good sources
Animal   Cheese, eggs, halibut, milk, salmon, shad, trout, tuna, veal.
Fruit   A poor source except for dried peaches.
Grains, nuts, seeds   Bread (enriched), cornmeal (enriched), mixed nuts, peanut butter, rice (enriched), wheat bran, wheat flour (enriched).
Vegetables   A poor source.

Selection   Canned, frozen, and dried products lose little of their niacin content (less than 20 percent) when compared to the rest of the B-complex group. Cereals lose close to 90 percent, but they are usually enriched with niacin.

PANTOTHENIC ACID

Through the years this vitamin has been given a number of names, including vitamin B_2 and B_3. Now it is commonly known as *pantothenic acid,* stemming from the Greek word *pantothen,* which means "everywhere." And truly, it is found everywhere, in all living cells of animals and plants, so deficiencies are rare. In humans the highest concentration occurs in the liver and kidneys. A certain amount is synthesized in our own bodies by the bacterial flora of the intestines, yet we still need a daily supply because pantothenic acid is one of the water-soluble vitamins of the B-complex group.

Functions   For bodybuilders, pantothenic acid plays an important role, acting as a coenzyme to release energy from protein, fats, and carbohydrates. It is also essential to the synthesis of fatty acids, cholesterol, and steroids (fat-soluble organic compounds). Energy released in the breakdown of the fatty acids is used for the formation of adenosine triphosphate (ATP), the main source of energy for muscular work. By releasing this energy immediately without oxygen, it allows athletes to function without being directly dependent on a supply of oxygen. The reason for being able to produce a burst of strength when lifting heavy weights is due to ATP.

Pantothenic acid also stimulates the adrenal glands, producing hormones necessary for healthy skin and nerves. It is necessary to the synthesis of antibodies that fight infection. Working in a manner similar to that of the other B-complex vitamins, it is vital to the development of the central nervous system and improves the body's ability to withstand stress. Many people believe it helps to prevent their hair from turning gray. Their belief is based on reports that a lack of pantothenic acid caused premature graying in laboratory animals. This has not been proven scientifically with humans.

Deficiency symptoms   As mentioned earlier, this vitamin is distributed so widely in plant and animal foods that deficiencies rarely occur, but a low intake can slow down many of the metabolic processes. A deficiency, however, can be evidenced by dizzy spells, depression, weakness, headaches, digestive disturbances, and irritability.

Destroys vitamin or limits absorption Stress, tobacco, caffeine, alcohol, sulfa drugs, estrogen, heat, and sleeping pills destroy or limit absorption.

Toxicity Basically, pantothenic acid is nontoxic. Some individuals may react to above-average dosages by getting diarrhea or retaining water in their tissues.

Storage The pantothenic acid content in natural food is reasonably stable unless they are subjected to high temperatures. Flour should be covered closely and can be kept up to a year. Seeds and nuts keep best in containers stored in a cool place.

Processing effects Canned fruits and vegetables lose 49–80 percent of their pantothenic acid content, and canned seafood loses over 20 percent. The losses from home cooking are significantly lower since food is not processed with temperatures as high as those used in a manufacturing plant. Home cooking also has the benefit of less salt and other additives used in prepared food.

Best sources Brewer's yeast, cottonseed flour, heart, kidneys, liver, rice bran, rice polishings, torula yeast, wheat flour, wheat bran.

Good sources

Animal Beef, blue cheese, buttermilk, chicken, eggs, lobster, milk (skimmed), salmon.

Fruit Avocados.

Grains, nuts, seeds Brown rice, buckwheat flour, cashew nuts, peanut butter, pecans, peanuts, soybean flour, sunflower seeds.

Vegetables Broccoli, cabbage, corn, peas, peppers, potatoes, mushrooms.

Selection Because the loss of pantothenic acid is high during processing, foods containing this vitamin should be purchased in their most natural form. Canned vegetables like mushrooms lose almost 80 percent of their pantothenic acid content while all-purpose flour loses about 60 percent during the milling process. When buying peanut butter, try to find a market where you can grind it yourself from fresh peanuts. Most health food stores usually have one of these machines, and now many markets are beginning to follow their example.

PARA-AMINOBENZOIC ACID (PABA)

PABA was first classed as a vitamin; however, continued research proved it worked more like a chemical, stimulating the production of folic acid, one of the B-complex vitamins.

Functions   Found in almost all sources of the B vitamins, it acts as a coenzyme in the chemical breakdown and utilization of protein. In this manner it contributes to a healthy digestive system and the formation of red blood cells. Bodybuilders with sensitive skin may be able to tan in comparative safety by using lotions containing para-aminobenzoic acid, which acts as a sunscreen. It also helps to delay wrinkles by maintaining smooth and healthy skin. Some people believe it will stop their hair from turning gray, but this idea is based on experiments made on laboratory animals rather than on people.

Deficiency symptoms   Fatigue, depression, and digestive disorders are symptomatic of a deficiency of this vitamin, but they also can indicate a deficiency in other B vitamins, especially folic acid. Be aware that PABA has a neutralizing effect on sulfa drugs. Therefore, inform your physician when you are taking this vitamin and he prescribes medications containing sulfonamides.

Toxicity   Toxicity, caused by taking high dosages over a period of time, may cause nausea or vomiting. At present, however, high-potency preparations are available only by prescription, causing little danger from this source.

Sources   The best sources of PABA are beef liver, brewer's yeast, eggs, fish, lecithin, molasses, peanuts, and soybeans.

VITAMIN C

Many animals make their own vitamin C in the process of synthesizing the glucose from plants, but we lack the enzyme oxidase that allows for this conversion. Our source in its most common form is ascorbic acid, found in citrus juices, whole fruit, vegetables, and dietary supplements.

Even those who know little about the nature and functions of other vitamins take vitamin C supplements when they have a cold. Like vitamin A, however, it is most effective if taken upon feeling the first symptoms of a cold or flu instead of waiting until it sets in fully. A daily quota of vitamin C supplements does not make you immune to colds, but many people find it lessens the severity of the usual cold symptoms. Because vitamin C contains an antihistamine, it is sometimes effective in treating a number of respiratory infections.

Since 1970, when Linus Pauling, a chemist and Nobel Prize winner, wrote a book advocating the use of vitamin C to combat colds and the flu, many people began taking it in massive doses. Despite his advice, I find it more important to know *when* to take vitamin C and so avoid the risk of getting kidney stones or an iron storage disease—a distinct possibility when the intake of vitamin C is very high. From my experience as a bodybuilder, I find it better to take vitamin C supplements twice a day—before and after training—rather than in a single dosage in the morning. By taking half the recommended amount before going to the gym, you will find it easier to warm up. Vitamin C works as a lubricating agent by thinning the synovial fluid in the joints and thereby allows freer movement. When you train you lose vitamin C from sweating heavily. This should be replaced by taking the remainder of your daily quota 30–60 minutes after finishing your workout. In this way the vitamin remains in your system for a longer time because you are not sweating very much. Through the years I have found this system highly effective since it deals with the immediate needs of my body. This is a more rational approach to the use of vitamin C than is taking massive doses. After all, this is a water-soluble vitamin, and although a small amount is stored in the body through tissue saturation, most is eliminated in the urine and through perspiration within three or four hours.

Functions One of the chief functions of vitamin C is the formation and maintenance of collagen, a protein essential to the formation of connective tissue of the skin, bones, and ligaments. Collagen is high in amino acids; therefore, a lack of it delays healing of wounds and burns. Also, it maintains the strength of capillary walls and blood vessels that otherwise could rupture as evidenced when people bruise easily. Vitamin C is necessary for sound teeth, strong bones, and the formation of red blood cells. Research has shown that cholesterol levels in the liver and blood serum tend to rise when there is a deficiency in this vitamin, yet they go down when normal dosages are taken. The absorption of iron is increased when taken with vitamin C, and it serves as an antioxidant, protecting vitamins A and E and the polyunsaturated fats. The need for vitamin C increases when the body is placed under stress resulting from surgery, extreme fatigue, injury, very high or low temperatures, cigarette smoking, and exposure to toxic levels of heavy metals like cadmium, lead, and mercury.

Deficiency symptoms   Some early symptoms of a vitamin C deficiency are fatigue, shortness of breath, sore or bleeding gums, pains in muscles that come and go, tooth decay, and cracking at the corners of the mouth.

Destroys vitamin or limits absorption   Stress, smoking, and high fever, as mentioned above, will destroy vitamin C as well as antibiotics, cortisone, aspirin, and other painkillers when taken over a long period of time. Because a high concentration of ascorbic acid is found in the adrenal glands, the synthesis of steroid hormones causes a severe depletion in this supply. Air, heat, light, and alkalies such as baking soda are destructive to vitamin C found in our food.

Toxicity   An overdose may first result in a burning sensation while urinating. This may be followed by stomach cramps, diarrhea, and nausea. Massive doses can cause destruction of the red blood cells, formation of kidney stones, and certain iron storage diseases. Keep in mind that some or all of these symptoms may accompany a medical problem not related to vitamin toxicity.

Storage   The storage of foods containing ascorbic acid should be considered carefully because it is the least stable of all the vitamins, being easily destroyed by light, heat, and air. Refrigerating vegetables is essential, especially those with large, leafy areas like spinach, kale, cabbage, and Swiss chard. Buy vegetables in small amounts and use within a day or two. Tomato, orange, and grapefruit juices can be stored in a covered glass container in the refrigerator for several days without losing much of their vitamin content, but they should never be left standing on the kitchen table.

Processing effects   Because cutting vegetables releases an enzyme destructive to ascorbic acid, they should not be sliced or diced until directly before cooking. Then use as little water as possible, keeping the cooking pot covered closely, and serve the vegetables immediately when they are ready. Do not defrost frozen vegetables, but put them into boiling water as soon as possible. Even better, use a vegetable steamer to avoid the leaching out of vitamins in cooking water. It is also best to cook vegetables with the skin left on. Baking soda and iron or copper pans will destroy vitamin C.

Best sources   Acerola cherries, currants, grapefruit, green peppers, guavas, lemons, limes, mustard greens, oranges, parsley, rose hips, turnip greens.

Good sources

Animal   Very little from this source, except a fair amount from liver.

Fruit   Apples, bananas, blackberries, blueberries, cantaloupes, papayas, peaches, pears, strawberries, sweet potatoes, tomatoes, white potatoes. Three times as much tomato juice as citrus juice is needed to supply the same amount of vitamin C.

Grains, nuts, seeds   No good sources, except a small amount from sprouted grains and seeds.

Vegetables   Asparagus, beets, broccoli, Brussels sprouts, cauliflower, collards, dandelion greens, kale, lima beans, red cabbage, spinach, sweet potatoes, Swiss chard, watercress, white potatoes.

Selection   A key to the high content of vitamin C or ascorbic acid in fruits and vegetables is the amount of sunshine they receive. The longer a plant is exposed to the sun, the greater its content of this vitamin. The acerola cherry, for instance, is the richest natural source of vitamin C, containing 1,000–4,000 mg per 3½-ounce serving. It is grown in Puerto Rico and other Caribbean islands, having the full benefit of sunshine not blocked by a layer of smog or air pollutants. Unfortunately, the fresh fruit is available only in the Caribbean, but supplements made from the acerola cherry are available in most health food stores.

The skin color of oranges and grapefruit cannot serve as a guide to buying citrus fruits unless they are purchased in stores specializing in organically grown food. Dyes are injected into the skin of citrus fruits purchased in most supermarkets to give them bright orange and yellow colors that look attractive and appeal to customers. Try to select fruit with a thin skin that yields slightly under finger pressure. Oranges, lemons, and grapefruit with thick skin usually feel lightweight for their size because they contain less actual fruit than those of a similar size that are thin-skinned.

Preferably, juice should be made fresh from the whole fruit squeezed at home. If you need to purchase frozen products, however, check the label to be certain they are 100 percent pure juice without the addition of sugar or preservatives. Fruit-flavored drinks should be avoided. Even if they do contain fruit juice rather than artificial flavoring, the actual fruit content is usually under 10 percent—the rest is junk.

VITAMIN D

If you live in an area with an abundance of sunshine and open space such as found in California, Texas, and Florida, your body will form vitamin D just from staying in the sunshine, provided you are not wearing heavy clothing. The ultraviolet rays of the sun activate a type of cholesterol found in the skin, forming previtamin D. This takes place during a period of three days before entering the circulatory system as the vitamin itself. Bodybuilders who get enough sunshine have no need to increase their intake of vitamin D supplements even when they train. However, those with dark skin may need additional supplements because over 90 percent of the ultraviolet rays from the sun do not penetrate their skin and form vitamin D. A similar problem is encountered by those living in crowded cities like New York and Chicago where the ultraviolet rays are screened by fog and air pollutants like smoke and soot. A deep suntan maintained over some length of time will also decrease the formation of this vitamin in the skin.

Functions One of the more important functions relating to bodybuilders is regulating the metabolism of phosphorus and calcium, since lack of calcium in the diet causes cramps, and both minerals are necessary for strong bone tissue. Vitamin D also serves in the utilization of amino acids. When it is lacking in the body systems, the excretion of amino acids in urine is increased.

Deficiency symptoms Loss of appetite, unusual thirst, nausea, vomiting, and diarrhea may be symptomatic of a vitamin D deficiency.

Destroys vitamin or limits absorption Mineral oil and air pollutants.

Toxicity Large doses of this vitamin should not be taken as a matter of course but should be prescribed by a doctor. Overdoses can cause abnormal deposits of calcium in the muscles and circulatory system and irreparable damage to the kidneys.

Storage Canned and frozen foods can be stored safely without losing their content of vitamin D. Supplements are rapidly destroyed by air, light, and acids; therefore, you should keep them in tightly sealed, dark-colored bottles.

Processing effects Vitamin D is stable even when foods containing it are cooked over high heat. Being fat-soluble, no vitamin D is lost in cooking water.

Best sources Cod liver oil, smoked eel, tuna (packed in oil).

Good sources

Animal   Eggs, herring, kipper, liver, liverwurst, mackerel, milk (evaporated), pompano, salmon, sardines, whipping cream.

Fruit   No good sources.

Grains, nuts, seeds   Only cereals that are fortified or irradiated.

Vegetables   No good sources.

Selection   Because this is one of the fat-soluble vitamins, very little is lost in canned or frozen products. Most foods containing it are high in fat content, so it is better to depend on sunshine or supplements for an adequate intake.

VITAMIN E (TOCOPHEROLS)

In 1936 vitamin E was first isolated from wheat germ oil and named *tocopherol,* taken from two Greek words, *tokos* and *pherein,* which meant "to bear offspring." The "offspring" are eight tocopherols making up vitamin E with alpha tocopherol being the most important nutritionally. Like other fat-soluble vitamins, it needs a certain amount of fat for absorption in the body. Its chief storage sites are the muscles, liver, and fatty tissue, yet a large amount is also found in the heart, lungs, uterus, testes, and adrenal and pituitary glands.

Functions   Its importance to bodybuilders is based on the essential role vitamin E plays in the respiration of cells, forming muscle tissue. In addition, it strengthens membranes making up cell walls and, in doing so, works to increase your muscular strength. Acting as a diuretic, it helps lower blood pressure, an important factor for bodybuilders who gain too much weight and place stress on their cardiovascular systems. Since those using steroid drugs also run the risk of elevating their blood pressure 10–15 percent above normal, they may also benefit from taking vitamin E supplements daily. Anyone allergic to oil-base capsules can purchase the vitamin in water-soluble dry-base tablets. Bodybuilders may find their endurance increased through the use of this vitamin because it helps increase a supply of pure oxygen from the red blood cells to the heart and other organs.

In its role as an antioxidant, it prevents saturated fatty acids from forming toxic substances in the digestive tract as well as the oxidation of vitamin A, vitamin C, and ATP. Research with laboratory animals has proven that vitamin E works to protect their lungs from air pollution. Experiments are now being conducted to discover if the same protection is afforded humans. The opinion of nutritional authorities is divided on whether or not vitamin E helps restore male potency and increases fertility in males and females.

Deficiency symptoms   Deficiencies are not often seen because it is found in a varied assortment of foods from plant and animal sources. Also, a certain amount of the vitamin is stored in most body tissues for extended periods of time. A deficiency, however, can cause significant changes in the circulatory, nervous, and reproductive systems. Muscle degeneration can occur due to the rupture of red blood cells from having weak cell walls.

Destroys vitamin or limits absorption   Deep-fat frying in restaurants and fast food chains that use the same cooking oil over and over again will cause high losses in vitamin E. The excessive use of cod liver oil will limit absorption because it is high in unsaturated acids.

Toxicity   Virtually nontoxic when compared with the fat-soluble vitamins A and D.

Storage   Grain, seeds, and nuts should be stored in tightly covered containers because tocopherols are easily destroyed by light and oxygen. Let avocados ripen at room temperature before storing them in the refrigerator. They should be used within four or five days. Blackberries, like other fleshy berries, dislike moisture, so do not rinse them before storing in the refrigerator. Use the berries within two or three days because they tend to turn moldy.

Processing effects   Home cooking of foods results in almost no loss of vitamin E. Because they are insoluble in water, no E vitamins are drained off when vegetables are boiled. Keep in mind, however, that the water-soluble B vitamins they contain will be lost when the cooking water is drained off. High temperature used in deep-fat frying results in over 80 percent of the vitamin being destroyed.

Best sources   Alfalfa seeds, almonds, Brazil nuts, cottonseed oil, filberts, margarine, peanuts, pecans, safflower oil, sunflower seed oil, wheat germ oil.

Good sources
Animal   Butter, cod, crab, eggs, heart, liver, lobster, kidneys, salmon, shrimp, sweetbreads, tuna.
Fruit   Apples, avocados, blackberries.
Grains, nuts, seeds   Almond oil, corn oil, oatmeal, peanut oil,

rice bran oil, rye (whole grain), sunflower seeds, soybean oil, wheat flour.

Vegetables   Asparagus, beans, broccoli, carrots, celery, dandelion greens, escarole, kale, olive oil, spinach, tomatoes, turnip greens.

Selection   Buy only whole grain products because over 80 percent of the vitamin E content is lost through the process of milling grains. I have yet to see a product label indicating it was enriched with vitamin E. Avocados should be slightly soft if they are intended for immediate use, but firm if you plan on storing them over five days. Canned meat and vegetables have lost up to 68 percent of their alpha tocopherol content, and roasted nuts lose over 80 percent.

VITAMIN F

Vitamin F, consisting of unsaturated fatty acids and linoleic acid, is another of the fat-soluble vitamins. It does not play an important role in the nutritional intake of bodybuilders but is listed for your information.

Functions   Like vitamin D, it helps prevent muscular cramps by promoting the availability of calcium to the cells. It also breaks up cholesterol deposits on artery walls and aids in the transport of oxygen through the circulatory system to cells, tissues, and organs.

Deficiency symptoms   People having a high intake of carbohydrates may need to increase their intake of this vitamin. Deficiencies may cause acne or eczema.

Toxicity   No toxic reactions are on record; however, an excess can lead to a weight gain of fat, not muscle.

Sources   The best sources are cod liver oil, corn oil, pecans, safflower oil, soy oil, sunflower seeds, and wheat germ.

VITAMIN K

The chief function of this fat-soluble vitamin is producing prothrombin, a blood-clotting substance that prevents hemorrhages. If you are subject to nosebleeds very often, or notice that cuts take a long time to stop bleeding, I would suggest discussing the use of vitamin K with your doctor. Bodybuilders on steroids, which make the liver work overtime, may also want to investigate the use of this vitamin since it plays a role in maintaining a healthy liver. And, to a small degree, it also works in converting glucose to glycogen.

In addition to being found in foods and supplements, vitamin K is also manufactured in the body by intestinal flora. Yogurt stimulates the production of the flora, with only a teaspoon of yogurt necessary every few days to stimulate its growth.

Processing, destruction, toxicity, and deficiencies   Little loss of vitamin K occurs at normal cooking temperatures; however, all food should be fresh, with leafy vegetables stored no longer than a day or two in the refrigerator. It is easily destroyed by sunlight, rancid fat, aspirin, and radiation, with deficiencies evidenced by nosebleeds, hemorrhages, and colitis. Natural forms do not produce toxicity, but menadione, one of its synthetic forms, has caused jaundice.

Sources   Some of the best sources are asparagus, avocados, beef cooking oils, green leafy vegetables, kidneys, liver, nuts, oatmeal, seeds, turnip greens, and wheat germ oil.

VITAMIN P (BIOFLAVONOIDS)

Hundreds of different bioflavonoids make up the vitamin P group, over 30 of which are found in citrus fruits, giving their skin orange or yellow colors. The vitamin itself, however, is found in the white pulp and core that runs down the middle of citrus fruits. The only exceptions are tangerines, in which the highest percentage of bioflavonoids is found in the juice. Keep in mind that manufacturers of canned and frozen juices remove the white pulpy portion of citrus fruits because it gives a bitter taste to the juice.

Functions   Bioflavonoids play a role in reducing water accumulation in the tissues, and for this reason may be helpful to bodybuilders having a problem in this area. In this case bioflavonoids should be taken with vitamin C since they work best together and are not found in vitamin C supplements. Also, those having difficulty with the proper absorption of vitamin C should find C-bioflavonoid supplements helpful to their condition. Then they should be taken daily because both vitamins are water-soluble and not stored in the body. Bioflavonoids also serve to strengthen capillary walls and help prevent bruising that occurs in contact sports.

Deficiency symptoms   As bioflavonoids are such close companions of vitamin C, their deficiency symptoms are similar, being evidenced by fatigue, bleeding gums, cracking at the corners of the mouth, and fleeting muscular pain.

Toxicity   None of the bioflavonoids is toxic.

Sources   The best natural sources are whole citrus fruits. Other rich sources are apricots, broccoli, cantaloupes, grapefruit, green peppers, lemons, oranges, papaya, red wine, rose hips, tangerines, and tomatoes.

MINERALS

CALCIUM

Most of the body's supply of calcium—weighing 2-3 pounds— is found in our bones and teeth. The remainder is found in the soft tissues of organs such as the liver, stomach, and intestines and in our muscles. One of the greatest benefits I gained from an increased intake of calcium supplements was the prevention of cramps, especially during competition. I discovered the same was true for other bodybuilders. Whenever I entered a contest and saw one of them having a problem with cramps, I gave him calcium supplements. In most cases, his condition not only improved dramatically but disappeared entirely. Another important benefit provided by calcium is relieving the jangled nerves and tension suffered by every contestant getting ready to walk onstage. I generally take 3-4 mg of calcium daily for several weeks before competing and 4,000 on the big day.

Functions   In addition to the essential function of calcium in muscle contraction and relaxation, it is required to activate a number of enzymes needed to produce ATP for energy and to break down protein molecules. Calcium also serves as one of the agents necessary for blood clotting and releasing a number of hormones into the body systems. Working together with magnesium, it promotes cardiovascular health; working with phosphorus, it maintains strong bones and teeth. Its rate of absorption is increased by vitamin D either from your dietary intake or from the sun. Lactose, or milk sugar, will also increase absorption of calcium.

Deficiency symptoms   Deficiencies can occur when hard physical work is done in extreme heat. In such cases heavy sweating can cause a loss of over 100 mg of calcium in one hour. People with hypoglycemia may also suffer a deficiency, but they should check with their physicians before increasing supplementary intakes of calcium.

Extreme nervousness, a slow pulse, pains in the joints, and cramps are the main symptoms of a deficiency.

Foods that destroy or limit absorption of calcium   Excessive quantities of saturated fat, chocolate, spinach, beet tops, and rhubarb destroy calcium or limit its absorption. Vegetarians should be aware that the phytic acid contained in the bran of cereals can be destructive to calcium when cereal is a major part of their dietary intake. A deficiency of vitamin D inhibits the absorption of calcium significantly.

Toxicity   Although the ratio of phosphorus to calcium should be approximately one to two, athletes and others who exercise regularly and are in good health can increase their daily intake of supplements provided their supply of vitamin D is adequate.

Some people may get kidney stones from megadoses of this mineral.

Processing effects   Minimize loss of calcium in vegetables by leaving them in large pieces and cooking with steam or a small amount of water.

Best sources   Blackstrap molasses, cheese, bonemeal, bulgur flour. Cheese, one of the top sources of calcium, is high in fat, which causes a loss of definition. Therefore, bodybuilders may want to choose other sources of calcium.

Good sources

Animal   Bones of meat and fish, caviar, ice cream, milk, oysters, yogurt.

Fruit   Figs (dried), prunes, raisins.

Grains, nuts, seeds   Almonds, Brazil nuts, filberts, hazelnuts, soybean flour.

Vegetables   Collard leaves, kale, spinach, turnip greens.

CHLORINE

Many people are familiar with the controversy arising from the addition of chlorine to supplies of drinking water. Nutritionists argue that chlorine destroys vitamin E and intestinal flora, but government agencies deny these claims, stressing its role in preventing highly contagious diseases such as typhoid fever and hepatitis. While this battle goes on, we can focus on several other functions performed by this essential mineral.

Functions   Chlorine is essential to the formation of HCl found in digestive juices, thereby helping in the utilization of protein and the absorption of iron and the B vitamins. During the digestive process, it also works to break down starch molecules by activating enzymes needed to stimulate this procedure.

A number of nutritionists believe it plays a significant part in maintaining the resiliency of tendons and joints. If this is true, some consideration should be given to the utilization of chlorine. As bodybuilders, we place great strain on these tissues supporting our muscles, so keeping them in youthful condition is important. Quite frankly, however, I tried increasing my intake of chlorine without discovering any advantage.

Deficiencies   Pure vegetarians who exclude salt from their dietary intake can suffer a deficiency in this mineral; otherwise, an average daily intake of salt is sufficient.

Toxicity   If your kidneys are working properly, toxicity is unlikely. For your information, though, the symptoms of toxicity are lack of appetite, muscle cramps, and shallow breathing. This can occur from taking diuretics in excess or following prolonged diarrhea.

Sources   Chlorine is closely associated with sodium, being found in table salt and other foods containing salt, such as kelp, olives, and rye flour.

CHROMIUM

Although chromium is one of the essential trace minerals necessary for good health, I find it has no particular significance in bodybuilding. For your information, it works with other body substances in forming hormones, activating enzymes, and stabilizing nucleic acids. A hair analysis test, discussed elsewhere in the book, will indicate if you are low in chromium. A deficiency should be brought to the attention of your physician. Do not attempt to doctor yourself with any type of inorganic chromium salts since many are deadly poisons. The chromium found in more expensive multimineral supplements is safe.

COPPER

The most important function of copper takes place when it unites with protein to form the hemoglobin needed for oxygen-bearing red blood cells. It also serves as a coenzyme required for normal energy metabolism. The bones, tendons, and connective tissues of our body systems need copper for proper maintenance and development. The color of our skin and hair draws its pigmentation from this mineral. In addition, the utilization of iron requires a number of enzymes containing copper, and it is necessary to proper functioning of the brain cells.

I have experimented with increasing my intake of this mineral, but found no difference in my energy level or muscular development.

Destruction, deficiencies, and toxicity   Like many other minerals, copper is not easily destroyed by food processing. Severe deficiencies are rare and are usually due to some abnormal body function. Toxicity is almost nonexistent, resulting primarily from liquids that run through copper pipes or are stored in copper tanks.

Sources   It is distributed widely in many foods of plant and animal origin with raw oysters and fried liver containing the highest concentrations. Other good sources are avocados, black pepper, blackstrap molasses, brewer's yeast, cheddar cheese, cocoa, granola, green leafy vegetables, nuts, peanut butter, and wheat germ.

IODINE

Iodine is a trace mineral whose prime function is regulatory. Two-thirds of the body's supply is found in the thyroid gland located at the base of the neck, just above the collarbone. Here, hormones containing iodine work to control the rate of oxidation inside the cell membrane. In this way they regulate circulatory activity that affects muscle tissue as well as the metabolism of nutrients. By stimulating the function of nervous tissue, the iodine-containing hormones also speed mental reaction and increase energy.

Deficiency symptoms   Personally, I have never given much thought to my iodine intake, since I use salt and eat plenty of seafood—both good sources of this trace mineral. I know some people do have deficiencies if they live in areas where food is grown in iodine-poor soil, such as found in the Midwest, around the Great Lakes, and in the Pacific Northwest. Women, in particular, seem to have the deficiency evidenced by goiter, or enlargement of the thyroid gland. The best preventive measure is using iodized salt.

Destruction It should be noted that the absorption of iodine is curtailed severely when large quantities of cabbage, turnips, cauliflower, and kale are eaten raw. But when these vegetables are cooked, elements destructive to iodine are neutralized and cause no problem.

Toxicity Iodine found in salt and food causes no toxicity, but it can be hazardous when used as a drug.

Sources The best sources are blackstrap molasses, iodized salt, onions, and saltwater fish.

IRON

All the iron in the body is combined with protein to produce hemoglobin, the red-colored substance in our blood cells. Hemoglobin, consisting of 6 percent *heme* (iron) and 94 percent *globin* (protein), transports oxygen in our blood from the lungs to the tissues. Iron is also essential to the formation of myoglobin, another protein-containing substance found only in muscles. Here, it is stored for use until needed for muscle contractions. Iron also serves as one of the coenzymes essential to energy metabolism.

Because of its importance in transporting oxygen throughout the body, attention should be given to an adequate intake of iron, although I noticed no significant difference either by increasing or decreasing my daily intake. It should be noted that menstruating women tend to lose almost twice as much iron as men; therefore, women usually will have a greater need for supplements. Most humans can absorb 6–10 mg daily with vitamin C and HCl increasing the rate of iron absorption.

Deficiencies and destruction Most cases of toxicity are related to toddlers who take iron supplements intended for their parents. Large quantities of coffee and tea limit the absorption of iron and can lead to a deficiency. Coffee and tea drinkers were less subject to this problem when cast-iron cookware was still in use, since it increased the iron content of many foods having an acid reaction, such as tomato-based sauces and fruit. Today, the iron content of food can best be preserved by cooking meat in large pieces and plant foods in small quantities of water. A deficiency can cause anemia, evidenced by a pale skin, dizziness, abnormal fatigue, and shortness of breath.

Best sources Blackstrap molasses, clams, liver, oysters, wheat germ.

Good sources

Animal Beef, caviar, chicken giblets, eggs (yolk), heart, kidneys, sardines.

Fruit Apricots (dried), peaches (dried), prunes, raisins.

Grains, nuts, seeds Bulgur flour, nuts (mixed), rice (enriched), rice polishings, soybean flour, wheat flour, whole grains. *Note:* Cereals can decrease the absorption of iron due to their content of phytic acid, which inhibits enzyme action.

Vegetables Asparagus, lima beans (dried), herbs, spices, spinach.

MAGNESIUM

The conversion of blood sugar into energy is very important to bodybuilders, especially those in hard training. Magnesium, one of the essential minerals, helps to stimulate this conversion. In addition, it works to activate enzymes for the production of ATP needed for muscular energy as well as peptidases utilized for digesting protein. Calcium, sodium, potassium, and phosphorus are dependent on magnesium to promote effective absorption into the body systems. Vitamins C and E and the B-complex group are utilized better when the consumption of magnesium is within the recommended daily allowance. It has been found useful for relaxing muscle contractions and nerve impulses.

Foods that destroy or limit absorption of magnesium The absorption of this mineral is inhibited by megadoses of calcium and a high intake of foods such as rhubarb, spinach, and whole grain cereals. This should be given particular attention by pure vegetarians and those on Zen macrobiotic diets who eat only specific types of food over long periods of time. If they live in areas where magnesium is plentiful in the drinking water (hard water), they may be able to compensate for significant losses caused by their dietary intake. Overcooking foods in large quantities of water also can cause some loss of their magnesium content.

Deficiencies Because excessive amounts of alcohol are destructive to magnesium, many alcoholics suffer severe deficiencies of this mineral. Muscle spasms, loss of appetite, and hallucinations are some symptoms of a deficiency.

Toxicity   Magnesium has proved toxic when the kidneys cannot rid the body of an overload.

Best sources   Celery seed, cocoa (pure powder), coffee (instant), dill (dried), fennel, marjoram, peanut flour, sage, sesame seeds, soybean flour, tarragon, wheat germ.

Good sources

Animal   No good sources.

Fruit   Dried apricots and figs.

Grains, nuts, seeds   Almonds, Brazil nuts, cashew nuts, peanut butter, peanuts, wheat-soy flour.

Vegetables   Beet greens, blackstrap molasses, garbanzo beans, Swiss chard, turnip greens.

MANGANESE

Manganese is another of the trace minerals found in better grades of multimineral supplements. In my opinion, it serves no particular purpose in bodybuilding, yet it does help to activate a number of enzymes needed for the metabolism of proteins, fats, carbohydrates, and nucleic acids. When calcium is taken in excess it may interfere with the absorption of manganese. A hair analysis test can determine if your supply of this mineral is adequate. No toxicity from a dietary intake has been recorded.

PHOSPHORUS

Phosphorus and calcium are closely related, being found together in the blood serum throughout our body systems. To maintain a proper chemical balance, we need twice as much calcium as phosphorus. A deficiency or an overabundance of either mineral causes a disruption in the storage and utilization of the other. For example, when the amount of phosphorus we ingest goes up, our supply of calcium goes down. Usually, bodybuilders are high in phosphorus because (1) it is found in almost all foods, especially proteins: (2) the absorption rate of phosphorus is 70 percent as opposed to 25 percent for calcium: and (3) hard workouts draw on calcium reserves more than any other mineral. reserves more than any other mineral.

Although phosohorus is important to the stimulation of muscle contraction and the metabolism of fats, proteins, and carbohydrates, no physical changes were evident whether I increased or decreased my intake of supplements. However, it does serve a number of life-supporting functions since phosphorus is found in every body cell. The most important is the role it plays in the process of mitosis, for without it cells could not divide and build muscle tissue or any tissue needed to maintain and repair our bodies. Strong bones and teeth, enzyme systems, and the formation of ATP required for muscular energy are also dependent on phosphorus.

Foods that destroy or limit absorption of phosphorus   Keep in mind that the calcium-phosphorus balance is disrupted by the use of white sugar. Many food preservatives have a phosphate base that should be included as part of your phosphorus intake. Antacids taken over long periods of time can deplete your supply of this mineral, and excess magnesium and iron can make it ineffective.

Deficiencies   Because it is found in nearly all foods, deficiencies are rare, except among some vegetarians on diets low in dairy products.

Toxicity   No toxicity from phosphorus is known.

Sources   Among the top sources of phosphorus are cocoa powder, eggs, fish, meat, poultry, pumpkin seeds, sunflower seeds, and whole grains.

POTASSIUM

Approximately 5 percent of the body's mineral content is potassium, the most important element besides calcium and phosphorus. It is closely related to sodium in maintaining the acid-base balance of the body by transferring nutrients in and out of the cells. With potassium working within the cell membrane and sodium working outside, they maintain an environment permitting the free transfer of nutrients throughout the cellular system. Potassium also helps to relax muscles. By combining potassium with calcium, I noticed that muscular cramps were relieved faster than by taking calcium alone. Other functions of potassium are reducing high blood pressure and uniting with phosphorus to provide the brain with oxygen.

Deficiencies and limited absorption   Deficiencies can result from crash diets, drinking excessive amounts of alcohol or coffee, and intense sweating over a long period of time. Any one of these situations causes a high-level loss of potassium and can result in muscular weakness, poor reflexes, and irritability. Since potassium acts as an agent for relaxing heart action, a high intake of supplements can cause cardiac arrest. Fortunately, the absorption rate of potassium from food is over 90 percent, so very little is needed to supplement the amount found in our dietary intake.

Sources   The best sources of potassium include avocados, beef, blackstrap molasses, brewer's yeast, dried fruits, lima beans, nuts, poultry, raw vegetables, sunflower seeds, torula yeast, wheat bran, wheat germ.

SELENIUM

The importance of selenium as one of the essential trace minerals was discovered in the late 1950s. Since then, most research has been conducted on farm and laboratory animals. To date there is no evidence showing that selenium is helpful in bodybuilding. However, its use should be investigated by people working in areas where mercury and cadmium are used in manufacturing processes. The body tissues are offered a measure of protection from these poisonous minerals by supplements containing vitamin E and selenium working together as antioxidants.

Deficiencies, toxicity, and sources   Deficiencies can be indicated roughly by hair and fingernail analysis. In its pure form, selenium can be toxic. It is safe taken in multisupplement form and in natural foods having a high content, such as Brazil nuts, butter, brewer's yeast, lobster, torula yeast, and wheat germ.

SODIUM IN ALL ITS FORMS

Our intake of sodium is derived chiefly from three sources: (1) table salt added to food, (2) sodium compounds like monosodium glutamate, and (3) salt added to processed food. In addition, a relatively high amount is found in food from animal sources, such as dairy products, meat, fish, and eggs. Sodium, one of the minerals absorbed most quickly by the body, is found in our bones, body fluids surrounding cells, and cardiovascular system. Working along with potassium, it serves an essential role in aiding nerve stimulation and muscle contraction. It is also necessary for the absorption of carbohydrates and to maintain the water-acid

balance in our body systems. Any excess not used by the body—
normally about 90–95 percent—is excreted in the urine. The
average person requires a minimum of .2 grams or 1/10 of a
teaspoon of salt daily. Bodybuilders and other athletes who sweat
profusely while training need about 2 grams or approximately 1
teaspoon per day.

Some bodybuilders have a tendency to eliminate salt from their
diets to prevent water retention. And a number of my chiropractic
patients have said, "My doctor told me salt is not good for me."
Since salt serves important functions as mentioned above, I find it
difficult to believe any doctor would advise a healthy person to
eliminate it completely. Problems do not stem from the ordinary
use of salt in cooking fresh, simply prepared meals, but from its
excessive use in food processing and junk foods, which are
discussed later. I never had any problems with water retention
when adding a little salt to my food or using it in cooking. An
excessive amount, however, will interfere with the absorption and
utilization of protein foods and may cause a loss of potassium.
Keep in mind that some exceptionally high sources are Canadian
bacon, green olives, and canned shrimp, which contain approximately ¾ gram of sodium per ounce. Luncheon meats, processed
cheeses, cucumber pickles, corned beef, and cured pork are also
high in sodium, having about ½ gram per ounce.

Many hardworking athletes who sweat heavily are so concerned
with lacking salt that they pop salt tablets into their mouths
without understanding their effect on the body. Those tablets
contain salt in a highly concentrated form, forcing a large quantity
of fluid to be drawn into the stomach. Despite this excess fluid, the
tablets eventually have a corrosive effect on the stomach lining.
This damage can be prevented by being aware of the amount of
salt actually included in your food intake, making consumption of
these highly concentrated salt tablets unnecessary.

Next to sugar, salt is one of the most popular substances added
to foods, although it is disguised on product labels under a number
of different identities. The following will give you an idea of how
much salt you consume without knowing it constitutes an ingredient for preserving, emulsifying, and adjusting the acidity of food.

Table salt (sodium chloride)   If manufacturers could refrain
from habitually using table salt in canning and processing.foods,
we could control its use better than other forms of sodium. Since
childhood we have all seen a saltshaker standing on the kitchen

table and are generally aware of the amount sprinkled on our food. As you have probably noticed, some people always add salt to their food; others never do. This certainly indicates that not all taste buds are the same. Yet, manufacturers of canned and frozen foods assume everyone has a uniform taste for the quantity of salt added to their products. Fortunately, it is now possible to buy canned vegetables and fruits that are salt-free. Usually they are found in the supermarket along with diet foods and are also stocked in most health food stores.

Brine   The mixture of table salt and water that forms brine has been used for hundreds of years to preserve food by inhibiting the growth of bacteria. In this form it is used for making sauerkraut, pickles, pastrami, and corned beef. To prevent fruits and vegetables from darkening before canning or freezing, they are quickly dipped into a solution of brine brought to the boiling point.

Baking powder   Sodium is one of the reactive agents in baking powder that causes cakes, cookies, certain donuts, and quick breads to rise. Because too much baking powder would ruin the texture of these baked goods, its use is most often kept within reasonable limits.

Baking soda (sodium bicarbonate)   Used as a leavening agent similar to baking powder, sodium bicarbonate is one of the ingredients found in baked goods, particularly when they are made with heavier ingredients as found in fruitcake and carrot cake. Many cooks, especially in cafeterias, keep vegetables looking fresh and green on steam tables by adding baking soda to the cooking water. And, until the invention of patent medicines, bicarbonate of soda was commonly used as a cure for indigestion.

Monosodium glutamate (MSG)   This ingredient is highly favored in Oriental cooking, and restaurant chefs are usually generous in its use. Because many people suffering cardiovascular or other medical problems have become ill from MSG, a number of Oriental restaurants now offer a choice of many items prepared without it. MSG is also used in the kitchens of hotels, restaurants, and fast food chains and is packaged as a seasoning sold under several brand names.

Sodium alginate   The smooth texture of most ice cream is created by this sodium-based compound. Chocolate milk, whether skimmed or whole, is often given its velvety texture by sodium alginate.

Sodium sulfite   To achieve the brilliant red color of maraschino cherries and some glazed fruits, they are first bleached in a solution of sodium sulfite and then dyed with food color. The same compound is used to preserve some dried fruits such as figs and prunes.

Sodium benzoate   Bottled salad dressings, sauces, and a grand array of relishes are kept as "fresh" as the day they were made by using sodium benzoate.

Disodium phosphate   The compound serves as a emulsifier in most packaged cheeses and the percentage of disodium phosphate used is quite high. It is also found in a number of quick-cooking cereals and is used to adjust the acidity of chocolate, soda pop, and sauces like Worcestershire, A-1, and soy.

Sodium proprionate   Twenty years ago, cheese and bread became moldy within four to five days. Now, with the addition of sodium proprionate, some types of bread remain soft and mold-free for over two weeks. Many processed cheeses stay fresh for seven to nine days.

Sodium hydroxide   You may wonder why canned and frozen fruit is so cleanly peeled when you cannot do the same with fresh peaches, plums, apricots, and pears. Part of the reason is the blanching process, in which the fruit is plunged briefly into boiling water. Afterward the fruit is treated in a solution of sodium hydroxide, which softens and loosens the skin until it slips off. Both processes contribute to a high loss of nutrients in canned and frozen fruit.

Deficiency symptoms   It should be obvious, therefore, that deficiencies of sodium are rare. Keep in mind that heat exhaustion accompanied by heavy sweating over a long period of time can cause salt depletion. The symptoms are nausea, muscle cramps, and a headache.

Toxicity   Toxicity can occur when your body has adapted to a long-term salt-free diet and you abruptly begin eating foods high in salt content. Severe problems can also be caused by restricting water intake when having highly salted foods.

Sources   Foods high in sodium include bacon, bologna, bran cereal, corned beef, cornflakes, green olives, ham, lunch meat, Parmesan cheese, potato chips, pretzels, processed cheese, and sausage. Pretzels have approximately 70 percent more sodium than potato chips.

Foods low in sodium include almonds; most fresh fruit and fruit juices; most vegetables except beets, carrots, celery, and spinach; walnuts; and whole grains.

SULFUR

One of the nonmetallic elements found in every body cell is sulfur, often considered vital to maintain the body beautiful. Since its highest concentration is found in the hair, skin, and fingernails, it has gained a reputation for keeping skin clear and youthful, hair glossy, and fingernails strong. Many ointments and creams used for the treatment of skin problems, such as acne, contain sulfur. Bodybuilders who want to look their best onstage may want to investigate some of these products, which are sold in most health food stores.

Functions Sulfur helps the liver produce bile, a point of special interest to bodybuilders, since bile breaks down fat that causes a loss of definition. Personally, I found that sulfur made no difference, but not all constitutions are the same, so others may benefit from it. Because sulfur takes part in the metabolism of carbohydrates, it also serves a function in providing energy. Several amino acids contain sulfur, thereby closely relating it to protein synthesis.

Deficiencies and toxicity Deficiencies are rare because it is found in a wide range of foods. Organic forms of sulfur are rarely toxic, but synthetic forms taken in high doses can be dangerous.

Sources Some important sources include blackstrap molasses, brewer's yeast, cheddar cheese, eggs, lean meat, navy beans, nuts, poultry, salmon, sardines, wheat germ, and whole grains.

ZINC

In North America much of the soil is low in zinc, a mineral that governs many essential functions in our body systems. A high concentration is found in the fingernails, hair, skin, and prostate gland. Trace elements found in the liver help break down alcohol. Those who drink excessively are often deficient in this mineral because large quantities of alcoholic beverages flush stored zinc from the liver into the urine.

Since zinc serves as a component of approximately 25 different enzymes required for the digestion and metabolism of carbohydrates, proteins, and fats, it is of particular significance to bodybuilders. Also, studies have shown it helps in the absorption of vitamins, especially the B-complex group, with a resulting high level of energy. I have experimented with increasing my intake of zinc without gaining the benefit of increased energy, yet I regularly take supplements containing it to compensate for food grown in zinc-poor soil. For your information, I would like to add that some authorities claim it is also required for healthy-looking hair and skin.

Deficiencies, limited absorption, and toxicity Most deficiencies are caused by diets that focus on a few types of food and exclude others. Loss of appetite, increased fatigue, dull hair, and slow healing of wounds are some deficiency symptoms. Absorption is also inhibited by EDTA, a chelating substance found in canned foods that is used to preserve their color and "true" flavor. Toxicity can occur from taking megadoses or from food kept in galvanized containers.

Best sources Liver, oysters, spices, torula yeast, wheat bran.

Good sources

Animal Cheddar cheese, chicken (dark meat), crab, eggs, lamb, pork, tuna, turkey (dark meat).

Fruit No good sources.

Grains, nuts, seeds Granola, peanut butter, peanuts, popcorn, wheat germ, whole wheat flour.

Vegetables Lentil sprouts, peas, turnip greens.

5

DRUGS AND WONDER FOODS

Most of us are fortunate to be born with our body systems working in perfect harmony. For the first few years of our lives we subsist on simple foods, rejecting what we don't like and eating only when hungry. Instinct guides our appetite rather than the flashy campaigns of advertising agencies that are fighting to survive in a highly competitive field. As time goes by, we are influenced by the culture of peer groups, leaving us vulnerable to anything that promises a new life in a new body within a few days or weeks. On every side we are bombarded by propaganda that eventually makes us believe in a world full of miracle-packaged drugs and wonder foods. Eventually, we move toward a lifestyle based on psychological needs created by society instead of actual physical needs. In this way many of our instincts atrophy. We begin to lose the natural harmony of our body systems by depending on drugs as shortcuts to success, thereby also losing the ability to function at the top capacity required of championship athletes. Bodybuilders who have reached the top in their class are not dependent on drugs or wonder foods. The miracles they believe in do not come in packages but are framed on the concept of training hard and concentrating on healthful practices.

STEROIDS

Aside from rigid, ill-informed dieting practices, the most common problem in bodybuilding today is the taking of steroid drugs without regard for the possibility of damaging one's health beyond repair. Sure, we all want to be winners, and competition is good, driving athletes to discover their full potential, but the day we come to value winning over good health is the time to stop and take a hard look at the cost of becoming a champion.

I became a Mr. Universe winner before I knew that steroid drugs existed. As a matter of fact, there was little mention of steroids in bodybuilding circles until 1976, when articles regarding their use began appearing in bodybuilding magazines. By the 1980s, however, interest in steroids was widespread among bodybuilders, so several individuals involved in the sport began writing booklets on steroids and selling them at high prices. They found a ready market composed of bodybuilders and young kids training with weights.

I read a number of these booklets and was shocked by the inadequacy of the information they contained. Guidelines for the safe use of steroids during limited periods of time and *only* under medical supervision were lacking. And even worse, there was little mention of their dangerous side effects if used indiscriminately as suggested by trainers or friends. For example, boys just growing into manhood are liable to become sterile if their reproductive systems are permanently disrupted by the use of synthetic hormones. Young men who are anxious to achieve the muscle mass they associate with true masculinity should be aware that bodybuilders in the 1970s had far more spectacular muscles than they do today. As far as I know, steroids cannot be credited for building bodies that win competitions.

Currently, other dangerous practices have become popular with many bodybuilders who experiment with steroids as if they were doing nothing more harmful than making an interesting salad or inventing a mixed drink. Some take a number of different steroids, changing them from one day to the next; others mix several types together and take them at one time. They are remarkably unaware that combining different types of steroids causes an interaction, rendering them either totally useless or highly dangerous. Remember, steroids originally were developed to rehabilitate hospitalized individuals suffering from anemia, arthritis, bone and skin

At an informal lecture, Dr. Columbu tells listeners to use their heads, whether in using proper training techniques or in avoiding hyped-up shortcuts to nutrition.

disorders, and illnesses that weaken the body following surgery. In such cases every patient is under close medical supervision. Their condition is monitored constantly by highly sophisticated lab tests, enabling treating physicians to determine which steroid works best for each individual at a specific time. Even more important, these tests can track harmful side effects caused by the drug, so it can be withheld before seriously impairing body tissue. For these reasons, a bodybuilder will *never* become an expert on steroids by trying different mixes and potencies on his own body. Most likely, he will die first. Already a number of deaths in bodybuilding due to the side effects of steroids have been reported.

I try to discourage people from taking steroids for another reason in addition to the one just discussed. As you can imagine, I have come to know a great number of bodybuilders all over the world. Those who became champions did not take steroids during the first years they were training, so they never developed a dependency on them. More precisely stated, by taking steroids in the beginning, you establish a dependency on drugs instead of the hard training that builds strength, endurance, and self-confidence.

In addition, be aware that steroids throw off body harmony as directed by the endocrine system, composed of eight glands working with the nervous system to coordinate body activities. Of the eight glands, normal functioning of the parathyroid is of vital importance to bodybuilders because it controls distribution of calcium throughout the body. Steroids force the parathyroid to overwork, thereby drawing calcium from the bones for use in muscles of the heart and other organs. This results in a calcium deficiency in the bone tissue, rendering them spongy and susceptible to fracture as well as causing tendons under stress to tear from bones. If you are given a blood test to determine the calcium content of your body, the high amount found in the blood will lead to an incorrect diagnosis. When too much calcium is drawn from bone tissue into the bloodstream, lab tests incorrectly indicate that an abnormally high concentration of calcium is present in your entire body. Based on this assumption, the doctor will advise you not to take calcium when you are actually suffering a deficiency and should increase your intake. Since the thyroid gland is closely connected to the parathyroid, it is also overstimulated by steroids, especially if individuals are taking thyroid supplements. All these problems and their consequences must be considered before embarking on self-directed experiments with steroids.

Having discussed the dangers of using steroids, I would now like to set forth a number of guidelines for their use under *controlled* conditions. My suggestions are not addressed to beginners, for the reasons stated above, but to those who have been in training for a number of years and have reached top levels in bodybuilding. If you decide on taking steroids at this point, they may give you an edge; however, this varies among individuals. Once you've reached the top, your experience in hard training and good nutrition has formed the groundwork for doing anything you want.

In my opinion, steroids should be taken only under the following conditions:

1. Medical supervision is vital. Only a doctor can determine which steroids work best for you and have the least damaging side effects. The doctor will monitor your condition by taking blood tests, measuring blood pressure and water retention, taking your pulse rate, and observing changes in behavior.

2. After the doctor determines which steroid works best for you, it should be taken on a limited basis. The first time, it works best if taken from five to eight weeks before competition. Thereafter, you should wait a year before taking them again for optimum results, reserving their use for the time prior to the most important competitive event.

Optimum results from steroids also depend on training your body beyond its usual capacity since your muscles need the additional stimulation. Although all your body systems will be working harder, the greatest stress is placed on the liver. For this reason, increasing your B-complex vitamin supplements is necessary, especially B_6 and B_{12}, which should be tripled from the amount taken previous to introducing steroids into your body systems.

After you stop taking steroids it is necessary to rehabilitate the liver, which was overworked while on the drug but functions much more slowly than normal when it is withheld. This will cause the liver to become fat-inflated, so the body very quickly becomes smooth. The process of rehabilitation requires double the amount of time you were on steroids. For example, if you took steroids for two months, returning the liver to its normal level of operation will require four months. During this period, I suggest increasing your intake of daily supplements, with an additional 3,000 mg of choline and inositol (usually found together in the same tablets or capsules) and 5,000 mg of lecithin.

Let me remind you again, however, that the road to becoming a champion is not paved with steroids and programs for rehabilitating the liver. It is based solidly on the right diet and training program done on a full scale. The remarkable progress made in bodybuilding during the past 20 years has been due to better systems of training, improved equipment, fine gymnasiums, and books geared to keep trainers and bodybuilders well informed. Knowledge is gathered scientifically with the aid of computers that can quickly gauge the results of lab tests for analyzing the mineral content of the body and foods causing allergies that weaken the system. Also during the past 20 years, research on vitamins and minerals has been increasing steadily so we have a more accurate understanding of their effects in relation to body systems. When a combination of all these elements is thoroughly understood and used together with common sense, the achievements of the body become incredible.

Of course, some bodybuilders will always be looking for some magic substance that can get them to the top without effort. They will waste years running around in circles, trying every available type of steroid without going to the gym and getting a great pump from a training session.

In conclusion, I offer the information that dianabol—found in tablet form—works better than other steroids. Yet I know many people have had bad reactions to it; therefore, it is essential to have a doctor evaluate any steroids you may select. Because dianabol has side effects similar to those of other steroids, the following is quoted from the *Physician's Desk Reference* on the problems that can result from its use.

CONTRAINDICATIONS: Hypersensitivity; male patients with carcinoma of the prostate or breast; carcinoma of the breast in some females; pregnancy, because of masculinization of the fetus; nephrosis of nephrotic phase of nephritis [kidney problems].

ADVERSE REACTIONS IN MALES: *Prepubertal:* Phallic enlargement; increased frequency of erection. *Postpubertal:* Inhibition of testicular function; oligospermia [decrease of spermatozoa in seminal fluid]; gynecomastia [abnormally large mammary glands in the male, sometimes may secrete milk].

ADVERSE REACTIONS IN FEMALES: Hirsutism [growth of body hair]; male pattern baldness; deepening of the voice; clitoral enlargement; menstrual irregularities; masculinization of the fetus.

ADVERSE REACTIONS IN BOTH SEXES: Increase in blood pressure; nausea; fullness; loss of appetite; vomiting; burning of the tongue; increased or decreased libido; acne [especially in females]; inhibition of gonadotropin secretion; jaundice; liver dysfunction.

CAFFEINE

The brain and central nervous system are both affected by caffeine and amphetamines, which act to delay fatigue by increasing mental and physical activity. This forces the body to use emergency reserves that should be replenished by rest. Physiologically, caffeine triggers a flow of stimulating chemicals from the adrenal glands into the bloodstream, causing blood sugar levels to rise. This causes blood vessels to constrict and can raise the blood pressure as much as 10 percent. The pulse rate slows down slightly.

The pros and cons of drinking coffee in relation to heart attacks have gone on for years. Some people in medical research claim that people who drink from one to five cups of coffee a day stand a 50 percent greater risk of heart attacks than those who drink none. On the other hand, other major studies have shown no link between coffee drinking and heart problems. One study showed that people who drank coffee were more likely to survive heart attacks than nondrinkers because caffeine serves as a mild stimulant.

In view of these conflicting opinions, healthy individuals should follow a course of moderation in drinking coffee and pay close attention to its reaction on their own body. Coffee does increase the output of stomach acid in the urine, and the excretion of magnesium is more than quadrupled. A magnesium deficiency will cause nervousness, tension, and hangover jitters similar to those brought on after a night of drinking heavily.

Some people who are more prone to coffee jitters than others try to avoid the problem by drinking decaffeinated brands. They should be aware that the caffeine is removed by using methylene chloride, a solvent that can cause cancer when taken extensively. Although the methylene chloride is rinsed away from the coffee beans, a residue still remains, and is potentially dangerous when ingested continuously over a long period of time.

Recently, a process using steam to remove caffeine from coffee without leaving dangerous residues like methylene chloride was developed in Switzerland; however, this product is high-priced and not normally stocked in most markets. Since espresso is also made by steaming, a great deal of the caffeine is dissipated along with the steam, making it safer to drink than regular coffee, which is perked or kept hot for long hours in coffee shops and restaurants. Being steamed quickly under pressure, espresso is low in acid as well as caffeine.

If you are particularly susceptible to the caffeine in coffee, take note of the fact that caffeine is found in more than 160 other plants and used in a number of drugs, food items, and beverages. Tea, with the exception of herb teas labeled "no caffeine," contains almost as much of the stimulant as coffee. It is also found in soft drinks, chocolate, stay-alert tablets, prescription drugs for headaches, and Anacin, Excedrin, Midol, and aspirin.

CIGARETTES

Most cigarette smokers have a tendency to ignore the warning found on every pack of cigarettes, "The Surgeon General has determined that cigarette smoking is dangerous to your health." They also ignore the well-publicized connection between smoking and lung and bladder cancer, chronic bronchitis, and emphysema. Physiologically, nicotine stimulates the sympathetic nervous system and triggers overconsumption of oxygen by the heart, making it a related cause of heart disease. Studies conducted at the University of Massachusetts established that smoking a pack and a half a day is the yearly equivalent of radiation doses from 300 X rays. Other problems related to smoking include a rise in cholesterol levels and a susceptibility to bacterial infections and colds. Every cigarette destroys 15–20 mg of vitamin C needed to maintain the strength of capillary walls and blood vessels.

MARIJUANA

Individuals who feel they have escaped the dangers of cigarette smoking by switching to marijuana should examine the harm caused by their new habit. One joint of marijuana contains as much tar as 100 cigarettes, and the body retains 30 percent of its active agents for a week. No other drugs or medications are known to remain in the body for this length of time. Of the portion remaining, 70 percent lingers in the body longer than the second week. Damage occurs chiefly in the autonomic nervous system and the brain, altering all body controls and thinking centers and causing atrophy of the brain and muscles when individuals are heavy users. Marijuana is also known to cause greater lung damage than cigarettes.

ALCOHOL

A controversy has always existed regarding the damage versus the benefits of alcohol. Let me preface my discussion of the conflicting viewpoints by stating that the best drink in the world is fresh water. It enables the body to absorb and convert all foods into nutrients and is essential to getting rid of waste products. Bear in mind that alcoholic beverages do not constitute part of your liquid intake because the fluid content is necessary to transport the alcohol itself. In addition, one shot of hard liquor, such as gin, rum, or vodka, requires an eight-ounce glass of water taken with it to prevent dehydration of muscle tissue.

Hard liquor is also high in calories due to its alcohol content, which converts to sugar in the body. Each shot contains approximately 100 calories with a carbohydrate value of 25 grams, which must be included in your minimum required intake of protein, carbohydrates, and fats listed in Chapter 3.

Many individuals use hard alcohol to mask conflicts, escape reality, or avoid coping with reality. In these instances, they bring on more serious problems, such as degenerative diseases of the heart, liver, and blood vessels. An excessive intake of alcohol cuts off the supply of oxygen to the brain, killing a large number of brain cells, which are irreplaceable because they are incapable of reproducing. Many people who drank excessively for over 25 years had brains that were four pounds lighter than normal. For these reasons I do not recommend hard liquor.

Beer and wine, however, are favorable when consumed in moderation because they are lower in alcohol content and less sugar-concentrated. A full bottle of beer, for example, contains 70–120 calories, depending on whether it is light or regular beer. The alcohol content ranges between 3 and 6 percent, making it low in sugar, a prime consideration for bodybuilders.

The alcohol content of wine is about 18 percent for sweet and 12 percent for dry varieties. Four ounces of sweet wine contains approximately 70 calories; the same amount of dry wine has about 40 calories. During the last few years, research has shown that wine is one of the best drinks for promoting the digestion of fats and proteins because it contains over 300 enzymes. The drier the wine, the higher its content of enzymes. Beer contains only a few, derived mainly from brewer's yeast and malt barley.

In summary, the body well utilizes a small amount of alcoholic beverages, which should be kept at a minimum, preferably limited to one four-ounce glass of wine with lunch and another with dinner.

STARCH BLOCKERS

The most recent "miracles" for those wanting to maintain a weight loss are antistarch pills, sold under a number of different brand names. In essence, they allow the consumption of bread, pasta, and other starches without concern for their caloric content. The active ingredient in the starch blockers is a kidney bean extract formulated to stop the action of enzymes that process starch during digestion. Lab tests on animals have proved the blocking action is harmful since it can permamently damage the pancreas. This organ will try to overcompensate for the blocking action by producing more and more enzymes until it works itself to death.

THYROID MEDICATION

Many bodybuilders trying to lose weight are indiscriminate in their use of thyroid medication. They little realize that an over-stimulated thyroid gland causes a loss of muscle tissue at the same rate as fat. Because this gland controls the speed of all cellular processes, it is not selective in banishing fat rather than muscle for the convenience of bodybuilders. In addition, thyroid medication has the harmful effect of also stimulating the parathyroid gland, controlling the calcium content of the bones. When stimulated,the parathyroid draws calcium from the bones into the blood tissue. Remember, a calcium deficiency can lead to muscle spasms and cramps during training and a decrease in performance. The hyperactivity most often associated with taking thyroid drugs is not the hallmark of a champion.

GLANDULAR SUPPLEMENTS

Many bodybuilders claim they are helped greatly by glandular supplements. I find that taking them makes no difference to people with normal glandular functions. For some of my patients who are sluggish, tired, and weak, however, I do recommend taking the supplements because they often make them feel better. The need for glandular drugs seems to vary among individuals, and changes during different periods of their lifetime.

WONDER FOODS

In truth I have never found any food more wonderful than eggs, and my opinions regarding their value are stressed throughout this book. Many young bodybuilders, however, are particularly vulner-able when it comes to believing myths created to sell certain food products at high prices. For example, one myth popular in bodybuilding circles a few years ago gave credit to the stimulating effects of Siberian ginseng for the superior performance of Russian athletes. Because anything with an exotic name seems to hold magical qualities, especially if you are young, I tried some but failed to discover any benefits. A short time later I went to Czechoslovakia as a participant in a weightlifting event also attended by a number of Russian athletes. Since a few spoke German, I took the opportunity to question them about the stimulating properties of Siberian ginseng I somehow was unable to realize. They shrugged their shoulders, saying they couldn't advise me since Russian athletes never drank the stuff. So, another myth died and was set to rest.

Spirulina, produced from a blue-green alga, has been touted as a miraculous energy-boosting substance. Although it is reported as being higher in protein than any other natural food, I am of the opinion that there is more protein in one egg than an entire bottle of spirulina. For this reason, it is totally useless for bodybuilders.

The same holds true for bee pollen, advertised as an age-retarding and rejuvenation food from the male germ cell of the plant kingdom. Some people may derive benefits from its supply of vitamins, minerals, enzymes, and steroid substances, but I tried bee pollen without discovering any.

Other items with a reputation among bodybuilders for being helpful are wheat germ for regulating body processes and wheat germ oils for preventing dry skin. I have tried both and can report only that their reputation is vastly overrated.

I realize that many individuals will try these products and other wonder foods to determine their value as I once did. Investigating myths for oneself is part of the learning process that leads every potential bodybuilding champion to eventually discard myths in favor of a few basic principles of sound nutrition and a good training program.

MODERN NUTRITIONAL TESTS

Before putting your faith in any drugs, medications, or wonder foods that promise to improve athletic performance, I strongly advise that you take a few simple tests that can determine chemical imbalances in the body, food allergies, and similar dysfunctions that drain energy and inhibit muscular development.

CYTOTOXIC TESTING

At the Columbu Chiropractic Center we are currently involved with several doctors working on cytotoxic testing. This is a process of evaluating specific foods and chemicals that damage the body systems by placing them under constant stress to combat toxic foods and substances. For example, when the blood tests of 1,000 adult patients were evaluated, we discovered that a majority were allergic to dairy products, though their nutritional value is first-rate. Milk and cheese are high in vitamin A and calcium, and yogurt helps regulate bacteria in the colon. Certainly, babies and young children need milk because serious conditions pertaining to growth and bone formation result when too little is consumed. Children thrive on milk, while many adults suffer allergic reactions due to a difference in their digestive processes. The young have an abundance of rennin, an enzyme that curdles milk, causing the protein to precipitate so it can be acted on by pepsin, another enzyme in the upper half of the stomach. Due to a limited production of rennin inhibiting the proper digestion of dairy products, many bodybuilders have problems with gaining definition because they accumulate a layer of fat beneath the skin. Some also suffer from headaches and sinus problems from an improper assimilation of the nutrients found in dairy products.

Cytotoxic tests are used to determine allergies to more than 250 food items and chemical substances. The majority of people are allergic to 28 or more of the items tested, with dairy products constituting the highest rate of food intolerances. The second-highest are chocolate and cola, followed by corn and citrus fruits. The actual process of cytotoxic testing entails a study of the interaction of your white blood cells with powdered extracts of specific foods, such as milk, onions, garlic, beef, mushrooms, and sugar. When microscopically examined in the laboratory, the white cells clump together if you are allergic to the food being tested. As far as I know, these tests have an accuracy rate ranging between 75 and 80 percent—far higher than others in which allergies are tested by scratching the skin to place a tiny amount of each suspected allergen underneath.

HAIR MINERAL ANALYSIS

A hair mineral analysis is an excellent indication of the balance of minerals in the body. Although this test is not geared to diagnosing or treating medical conditions, it does determine the lack of specific nutrient minerals and trace elements. In addition, it can indicate the extent of your exposure to toxic pollutants, such as cadmium, arsenic, lead, mercury, and aluminum, which are often present in the environment in which you live or work. Your hair more accurately records minerals stored in the body than a blood test or urinalysis. When the results of a hair mineral analysis are interpreted by a nutritional practitioner, your diet and intake of supplements can be modified to correct mineral imbalances.

Other tests can be performed to determine your vital lung capacity and the composition of your body, showing the amount of lean and fat weight. As mentioned earlier, a blood analysis testing your liver function should be taken every four weeks when you are on steroids. Also, a urinalysis done at the same time can provide information that gives evidence of dysfunctions in your body systems before they get out of hand.

6
EATING FOR SUCCESS

Each year I receive thousands of letters from bodybuilders and other athletes around the world, requesting information on my dietary habits and intake of food prior to competitive events. Only a few answers can be given in a letter. It takes the scope of an entire book to explore fully the basis for my attitudes, opinions, and personal development in relation to nutrition. Remember, success is achieved not only by following the example of another, but also by understanding his reasons for pursuing a particular plan of action. Therein lies the power and self-mastery needed to overcome obstacles, outmatch competition, and become an expert or champion in any field.

My serious training for the Olympia started 8–10 weeks before the contest when I concentrated on working with full power. Careful attention was paid to my diet since mistakes could be costly, leading to a weight gain or to a loss of definition. During this period, when I trained from two to four hours a day, I increased the number of my daily meals. When bodybuilders are training an average of three hours per day for a contest, their meals should be increased from three to four or five daily, depending on the individual. Study the diets in this chapter, which were designed to maintain top shape without loss of energy. Minor alterations are allowable to suit your taste and needs. The emphasis on hydrochloric acid tablets ensures proper digestion of nutrients, one of the most important elements in a bodybuilding diet.

EIGHT TO TEN WEEKS BEFORE COMPETING

I usually began the day at about seven or eight with a breakfast of three or four eggs and a small piece of dry toast. Immediately afterward I took my vitamins and minerals. Four days a week I ate a large piece of fish for lunch with a baked potato or rice, most often having the potato because it is more nutritious. I varied the menu on three days with beef, veal, and liver. The meal was accompanied by a glass of wine and a small salad. String beans or a small tomato might be included several times a week. An hour later I ate two pears or only one apple because apples have a higher caloric value.

Dinner was approximately the same but never included meat other than chicken, to keep my intake of protein high and fat to a minimum. Fish was always the preferred item.

Although I trained at different hours of the day—in the morning, sometimes at noon, or in the evening—I carried a pound of grapes to the gym, eating them as I went along. This was very important because grapes provide a great deal of energy. I prevented any weight gain by having the grapes before a heavy workout, which burned off the calories. During this time I stopped eating nuts and seeds. I do not recommend them when preparing for a competitive event since they are high in calories and do not provide the immediate energy that is characteristic of grapes.

In the evening, when all the hard work of training was over, I had a glass of beer, which relaxed me, relieving tensions so I could fall asleep easily. Through the day I drank a great deal of water, especially when training at the gym.

TWO WEEKS BEFORE COMPETING

At this time my diet became more restricted. It was similar to the diet just described, with a few important exceptions. I eliminated bread and rice and cut down to one baked potato a day. I continued eating three or four eggs and alternated having fish or chicken every second day. I had fruit only before going to the gym and at no other time. My intake of vitamins and minerals was increased by one-fifth or one-fourth of the usual amount.

DAY BEFORE COMPETING

The biggest change in my diet always occurred the day before competing, when I started eating foods higher in carbohydrates than in protein. During the 25–40 hours preceding the contest, I felt it was essential to accumulate as much energy as possible, and this can only be accomplished with a diet high in carbohydrates. I then began eating two slices of bread, two or three baked potatoes, fruits, and vegetables, as well as three eggs, fish, and chicken.

DAY OF COMPETITION

In the morning, about two hours before the prejudging, I had two eggs, potatoes, and bread. When I left for the prejudging I took along a bag of fruit. Since there are several free hours between events, I would return to my room and eat a small quantity of fruit to provide a high level of energy. This plan helped me tremendously.

When the prejudging was over I ate beef for lunch. As mentioned earlier, beef protein contains more fat than fish, so it supplies a little more energy. Also, on the day of the actual competition, I no longer felt it necessary to eat fish. So, for lunch I had beef accompanied by a baked potato. Incidentally, I do not recommend eating the potato skin. Poisons are used to kill underground pests, such as worms, when the plant is growing, and a residue may remain even when the potatoes are washed and scrubbed. The afternoon of the contest, I took along another bag of fruit to build up energy before entering the evening competition. After the event was over I ate another small meal.

AFTER COMPETING

One mistake I made when competing in the Mr. Olympia two years earlier was eating too much after the contest was over. My stomach had become small after two months on a diet of concentrated protein such as fish and eggs. Since the stomach needs time to expand slowly, you should not eat large meals directly after competitive events.

Although this photo was posed in fun, Franco once regretted overeating after a major contest.

Having learned my lesson, I began the day after the next Mr. Olympia competition with a breakfast of two eggs, a glass of freshly squeezed orange juice, and a little more bread than before. For lunch I slightly increased my intake of carbohydrates. In this manner I gradually worked my way back to a normal diet, preventing any drastic change in weight and accumulation of fat. Most bodybuilders gain weight after a contest because they overeat outrageously and then suffer digestive problems.

As I began to taper off my rigorous training schedule, I also started adapting to a decreased intake of protein, which should be eaten in proportion to the amount of time spent working out.

Although I always stick to the rule of eating protein foods first and salads and sweets second, I do have favorite dishes just like everyone else. Under normal conditions I try to alternate them as much as possible. I try to eat poultry one day, fish on the next, and various meats on the days following. I love potatoes and spaghetti fixed in a number of different ways. The spaghetti itself should always be cooked *al dente* with a sauce of freshly cooked Italian tomatoes made without tomato paste. Real Italian tomato sauce is made thick by being cooked until all the water evaporates. In this way the sauce clings to the spaghetti rather than settling at the bottom of a bowl or dish. Also, I am extremely fond of spaghetti with a green sauce made with basil.

When I am off training, potatoes are one of my favorite food items. I like baked potatoes with a little olive oil and salt, but never with butter or sour cream. Potatoes roasted in hot ashes are another favorite. I make a delicious salad by slicing boiled potatoes, mixing them with oil, vinegar, and a little salt, and letting them chill in the refrigerator for an hour. When I am off training, they make a side dish or light meal. I also slice boiled potatoes into a pan containing a little cold-pressed olive oil and fry them until a little browned. They taste terrific when accompanied with a glass of great Italian wine.

I make a number of dishes similar to those just mentioned, always using fresh, natural ingredients and keeping the combination of foods simple. I make it a point to avoid dairy products even in noncompetitive times. I don't eat many cooked vegetables, although I had them in abundance when growing up in Sardinia. I never have chocolate or other candy, pies, or sweets, but occasionally I indulge my taste for rum cake.

I do not like and never eat a number of food items, feeling they have no nutritional value and do not play a role in muscular development. These include hot dogs, hamburgers, butter, soft drinks, packaged crackers, and canned and frozen dishes. I have never used ketchup or mayonnaise. In a good Mexican restaurant I will order *carne asada,* but never tacos or burritos because of the high calories. Oriental food is not to my taste, and the amount of sugar added to flavor it contributes to weight gain. I enjoy having a glass of beer or wine but dislike hard alcohol, finding the taste unpleasant. I find mixed drinks like Bloody Marys particularly repulsive. I have never used artificial sweeteners; even thinking about them makes me feel sick to my stomach. Originally, they were made for diabetics, and I have always considered the possibility that they may be more damaging to the body than sugar.

EATING ON THE ROAD

When traveling, it is easy to be thrown off your normal pattern of behavior, training, and diet. Finding the right food in a market or restaurant is sometimes extremely difficult, so learn to be selective when traveling. Look for restaurants offering a large selection of fish dinners, and you will always find it easy to choose a nourishing, low-fat meal. Fish should always be your first choice, but when this proves impossible, select chicken or meat. Form the good habit of always leaving some food on the plate. In many restaurants meat is accompanied by foods of low nutritional value, so plates look full and impressive, giving people the feeling of getting their money's worth. This is a surefire way of getting customers to return to the restaurant again and again. As far as I'm concerned, however, the amount of food or its decorative presentation is not impressive when it lacks muscle-building value.

I always begin my meal by eating the meat, fish, or chicken before the baked potato. The chicken skin is always removed because it is high in fat content. If you are given French fries, eat only two or three pieces and leave the rest on the plate. Order vegetables plain. When they arrive already prepared with butter or sauce, don't eat them. For salads, oil and vinegar should be brought separately to the table and added sparingly.

After having traveled to many countries around the world, I found the best fish was served in American restaurants. Not only

Franco and Arnold in Japan.

do they specialize in cooking the best-quality fish, but they also offer an amazing variety that is freshly caught. The American system of transportation is far more efficient and organized than in foreign countries, with over 21 million trucks delivering food across the United States. The total number of trucks is higher than those in the rest of the world combined. The best, freshest fish in Europe will be served in countries close to seacoasts. In most European restaurants chicken and veal are extremely well prepared, and this is fortunate, since they are two of the best low-fat protein foods. When ordering beef or other cuts of meat, always specify that a lean cut be served.

Except for white rice, food in Oriental countries is usually low in calories and fairly nutritious because their main ingredient is vegetables, freshly sliced and cooked immediately before serving. Vegetables are not very satisfying, however, since they lack a significant quantity of protein, causing you to feel hungry again soon after eating a meal.

Always available in every foreign country are eggs, which contain the highest-quality protein and can even be prepared in your own room. The main food enemy to watch in other countries as well as in the United States is sugar- and fat-laden desserts. No matter how tempting they seem, avoid them and have a piece of fresh fruit instead.

HOW TO KEEP MUSCLES AND SKIN TONED

The key to keeping muscles and skin toned is based on keeping a low accumulation of fat under the skin in a very thin layer. Muscles lose tone when people overeat and gain too much excess weight, or lose weight too many times too quickly, or accumulate excess fat between muscles and skin. Avoiding dairy products is an important step toward keeping a low percentage of body fat. Just as essential is properly training the entire body with all areas stimulated equally to retain good muscle tone.

BANISHING FAT FOREVER

The best way to banish excess fat is simple—find out what makes you fat and eliminate it forever. In addition, try to maintain a low percentage of fat as long as possible. Every year this percentage is kept at a minimum accustoms the body to staying on a low-fat basis. I maintain a low percentage of body fat by constantly adhering to a habit of eating small meals, avoiding junk food and too many snacks between meals, and graciously refusing all fattening foods people offer me. Above all, I avoid all dairy products to avoid forming a layer of fat beneath the skin.

FEMALE BODYBUILDERS

All the diets in this chapter are good for both female and male bodybuilders. The difference is not in the type of food allowed but in its quantity, regulated by the amount of proteins, carbohydrates, and fats. This is found in the intake tables in Chapter 3. As discussed earlier, these diets differ from others found in books on nutrition and dieting. They are geared to the average person rather than bodybuilders in hard training who exercise regularly. For this reason, their diets and intake of vitamins and minerals differ. In general, female bodybuilders should take more vitamin B_6 to prevent water retention, more iron due to menstruating, and extra choline to maintain a low percentage of body fat.

Many women participating in competitive sports, such as the

Olympics, have a problem with amenorrhea or a cessation of menstruation. This seems to occur even if the women are not taking steroids. Some of the women I train reported this problem when their percentage of body fat dropped below 10–12 percent of body weight. Ideally, their percentage of body fat should be above 15 percent to prevent amenorrhea, although this level differs with each woman and will change during different times in her life. Many female athletes have said that their menstrual cycle resumes normally after slowing down on training and raising their percentage of body fat; however, this is not guaranteed. Because of this, I advise female bodybuilders to cut their training schedule and increase their percentage of body fat when they have missed their menstrual cycle for over two months. However, *the problem must not be ignored.* Amenorrhea and irregular menstruating cycles can also be caused by other factors, such as pituitary gland tumors, premature menopause, or an underactive thyroid gland. Women experiencing problems with irregular periods or amenorrhea should not attempt to diagnose the problem themselves or take the advice of someone working in a gym. To prevent serious problems from developing, have the situation evaluated by a gynecologist who treats female athletes and knows whether amenorrhea is related to an abnormality or to hard training and a low percentage of body fat. At the same time, inform the gynecologist if you are taking any steroids or drugs since they can also contribute to an irregular menstrual cycle.

For some women, estrogen therapy serves as protection against hypertension, bone fracture, and mineral deficiencies. On the other hand, many have adverse reactions to it, so I do not advise taking estrogen for the first time before a competitive event.

Birth control pills have been known to cause an imbalance in the body during training, particularly in the content of iron. They also contribute to water retention.

DIETS

I have prepared a number of diets, again in answer to thousands of requests. They are unlike others found in books on dieting and nutrition, being designed mainly for bodybuilders, although diets designated for an average bodybuilder may be used for other athletes and active individuals.

As you will notice on the food intake tables in Chapter 3, protein for competitive bodybuilders is emphasized more than the other nutrients, to provide maximum muscle gain. Fats are kept at the lowest possible level. The competitive bodybuilder's diets are not meant for use on a long-term basis, but for a limited period of time before competition, as discussed at the beginning of this chapter.

Noncompetitive bodybuilders will find less protein and more carbohydrates in their diets since a high intake of carbohydrates is necessary to provide energy for training. Their intake of protein was calculated for muscle gain in proportion to the amount of time spent working out.

MEASUREMENTS

Cooking units given throughout the book are based on standard American measures. The differences between American and English measures are listed below.

	AMERICAN	ENGLISH
Cup	8 ounces	10 ounces
Pint	16 ounces	20 ounces
Tablespoon	½ ounce	1 ounce

METRIC WEIGHTS

1,000 milligrams = 1 gram
1 ounce = 28.35 grams
4 ounces = 114 grams
8 ounces = 227 grams
1 pound = 453 grams

VOLUME MEASUREMENTS

3 teaspoons = 1 tablespoon
1 tablespoon = ½ fluid ounce
16 tablespoons = 1 cup or 8 fluid ounces
2 cups = 1 pint
2 pints = 1 quart

DIET FOR AVERAGE BODYBUILDER
Training up to 1 hour, 5-6 times a week

Breakfast	2 eggs any style
	1 slice bread
	1 glass orange juice or 1 serving fruit
	1 cup coffee
	1 glass water
Lunch	Any meat or ½ chicken
	1 baked potato or a small serving spaghetti without cheese
	1 glass wine or beer
	1 glass water
Snack	Fruit, nuts, seeds
Dinner	Fish cooked any way, except fried
	Vegetables
	Salad
	1 glass wine or beer
	1 glass water

DIET FOR NONCOMPETITIVE BODYBUILDER
Training 1-2 hours, 3-6 times a week

Breakfast	3 eggs any style
	1 slice bread
	1 glass orange juice or 1 serving fruit
	1 cup coffee
	1 glass water
Lunch	DAY 1
	½ chicken
	1 baked potato
	1 slice bread
	1 glass beer
	1 glass water
	DAY 2
	Steak
	Small serving spaghetti without cheese
	1 glass wine
	.1 glass water

DAY 3
Turkey or ½ chicken
Brown rice
Vegetables
1 slice bread
1 glass beer
1 glass water

DAY 4
Veal
Vegetables, preferably peas or beans or a
    baked potato
1 slice bread
1 glass beer
1 glass water

DAYS 5, 6, and 7
Repeat any of the menus given above.

Snack   Fruit, nuts, seeds

Dinner   Fish any style, except fried
Vegetables
Salad
1 glass wine or beer
1 glass water

DIET FOR NONCOMPETITIVE BODYBUILDERS
WITH SLOW METABOLISM

Breakfast   2 eggs any style
1 slice bread
½ slice pineapple
1 hydrochloric acid tablet
1 cup coffee
1 glass water

Lunch   Fish
1 baked potato
Salad
2 hydrochloric acid tablets
1 glass water

Dinner	Fish
	Salad
	1 hydrochloric acid tablet

Note: For hypothroid individuals, it is very important to have an early dinner. If possible, eat first and work out later, 1-1½ hours after dinner. Since training speeds up the metabolism rate, it will also promote a faster rate of food metabolization, causing food to turn into muscle rather than being stored as fat in the body.

DIET FOR NONCOMPETITIVE BODYBUILDERS WITH FAST METABOLISM

Breakfast	3 eggs any style
	2 slices bread
	1 grapefruit
	1 cup coffee
	1 glass water
Snack	Nuts, seeds
Lunch	½ chicken
	2 baked potatoes or spaghetti without cheese
	2 slices bread
	1 glass water
Snack	Tuna
	2 slices bread
	Fruit
Dinner	Fish
	Brown rice
	Vegetables
	Salad
	1 glass water
10 P.M.	Fruit

DIET FOR COMPETITIVE BODYBUILDER
Endomorphic Body Type: Fast Fat Loss
Use only during hard training due to the high percentage of protein.

Breakfast	3 eggs any style
	1 slice pineapple
	1 hydrocloric acid tablet
	1 cup coffee
	1 glass water
Lunch	Fish
	Salad
	Vegetables
	2 hydrochloric acid tablets
	1 glass water
Dinner	Fish
	Salad
	2 hydrochloric acid tablets
	1 glass water

Note: Eat ½-1 pound of fruit **only** 30 minutes before training.

DIET FOR COMPETITIVE BODYBUILDER
Ectomorphic Body Type: Weight Gain

Breakfast	4 eggs
	2-3 slices bread
	1 glass orange juice
	1 cup coffee
	1 glass water
Snack	Fruit
Lunch	Chicken or steak
	2 baked potatoes
	Vegetables
	Salad
	2 slices bread
	1 glass water

Snack	Nuts, seeds

Dinner	Fish
	Vegetables
	Brown rice
	Salad
	1 glass water

Note: Also, eat a large quantity of fruit 1 hour before training.

DIET FOR COMPETITIVE BODYBUILDER
Mesomorphic Body Type: Training 2-4 Hours per Day

Breakfast	3 eggs any style
	1 slice bread
	1 glass orange juice
	1 cup coffee
	1 glass water

Lunch	Any meat or ½ chicken
	1 baked potato
	Fruit, only after the meal
	1 glass water

Snack	Small portion water-packed tuna
	Nuts, seeds

Dinner	Fish
	Vegetables
	Salad
	1 glass water

Note: In addition to the fruit listed above, eat ½-1 pound of fruit 30-60 minutes before working out.

DEFINITION DIET FOR COMPETITIVE BODYBUILDER
Training 2 Hours, 6 Times a Week

Breakfast	4 eggs any style
	1 slice fresh pineapple
	2 hydrochloric acid tablets
	250 mg vitamin B$_6$
	1 cup coffee
	1 glass water
Lunch	Large portion fish any style
	1 baked potato
	1 glass water
Snack	20 g (1 tablespoon) water-packed tuna
Dinner	Fish any style
	Vegetables
	Salad
	1 glass water

Note: Eat ½-1 pound of fruit 30-60 minutes before going to the gym, no matter what time you train.

DIET #1 FOR OVOLACTOVEGETARIAN
BODYBUILDER

Breakfast	3 eggs any style
	2 slices whole grain bread
	1 glass orange juice
	1 cup coffee
	2 hydrochloric acid tablets
	250 mg vitamin B$_6$
	300-500 mg vitamin B$_{12}$
	1 glass water
Snack	Nuts, seeds
Lunch	2 eggs
	2 baked potatoes
	Vegetables
	1 hydrochloric acid tablet
	1 glass water

Snack	Nuts, seeds
5 P.M.	Fruit
Dinner	Beans, peas, or lentils 1 slice whole grain bread 1 baked potato Salad 1 glass water
10 P.M.	Fruit

DIET #2 FOR OVOLACTOVEGETARIAN BODYBUILDER

Breakfast	2 eggs any style Oatmeal 1 glass orange juice 1 cup coffee 2 hydrochloric acid tablets 250 mg vitamin B_6 1 glass water
Snack	Peanut butter 1 slice whole grain bread
Lunch	Vegetables Salad with garbanzo beans 1 slice whole grain bread 1 hydrochloric acid tablet 1 glass water
Snack	Dried fruit
5 P.M.	Nuts, seeds
Dinner	Lentil soup Vegetables Small serving macaroni without cheese Salad 1 glass water
10 P.M.	Fruit

Franco and his favorite foods.

FOOD TABLES

Figures given in the tables were calculated to simplify dividing or doubling amounts. For the most part, they were rounded off to the nearest whole number since fractions of percentage points are insignificant here.

Calorie counts are included in all the tables because many people are accustomed to using this measurement to judge foods. I have never counted calories and am strongly opposed to the practice. First of all, it is time-consuming. Second, it ignores the nutritional value of food in favor of an accounting method that leads to bad habits. People start saving calories to splurge on rich desserts filled with sugar while the needs of body systems go neglected. Certainly, calorie counting has obscured the nutritional components of food to such an extent that some people do not know the difference between carbohydrates and fats. And this is an important difference because fats will cause you to gain weight more than twice as fast as carbohydrates. You'll find that knowing the nutritional value of foods will help you lose or gain weight more successfully than knowing the calorie counts of foods.

Some items appear on more than one table to highlight nutritional values that might otherwise be overlooked if they were

mentioned only in one category. Grain foods, for example, are usually looked at chiefly in terms of their carbohydrate content, yet their value as a source of protein should not be ignored, and this is of special significance to vegetarians. The tables have also been arranged to accommodate vegetarians who adhere strictly to a diet of food only from plant sources.

Although some meat products, especially canned meat spreads, contain carbohydrates, the carbohydrate content is not listed. For the most part, an eight-ounce portion supplies less than two grams of carbohydrate. When the amount of carbohydrate *is* significant a notation to that effect is given. Unless indicated, it's assumed that no fat or oil is used in cooking, so be sure to account for it as well as for breading used in the preparation of fish or meat. Salad dressing must also be added according to the quantity used.

Only edible portions of food, without bones or seeds, are used in the weights given. Fruit peel is included only if usually eaten, but it is omitted from items such as oranges, grapefruit, bananas, and pineapple. Poultry weights are given without the skin because it is high in fat content. Weights for other meats assume that all visible fat has been removed. Gravies and sauces must be calculated additionally.

Omission of certain food items does not imply that they lack nutritional value, only that they are not good sources of vitamins and minerals.

PROTEIN FROM ANIMAL SOURCES: EGGS, FISH, GAME, MEAT, AND POULTRY

FOOD	QUANTITY	WEIGHT (GRAMS)	PROTEIN (GRAMS)	FAT (GRAMS)	CALORIES	PROTEIN ABSORBED & CONVERTED INTO MUSCLE TISSUE
Beef						
Chuck, pot roasted	8 ounces	227	25	44	496	68%
Corned beef	8 ounces	227	30	48	552	68%
Chili						
with beef & beans	1 cup	250	15	10	250	68%
without beef	1 cup	225	10	6	254	48%
Hamburger, broiled						
lean	8 ounces	227	35	22	338	68%
regular	8 ounces	227	30	44	516	68%
Kidneys, braised	8 ounces	227	35	15	271	68%
Liver, fried	8 ounces	227	40	20	340	68%
Round steak, lean, fried	8 ounces	227	45	27	423	68%
T-bone, porterhouse, rib, sirloin steak, broiled	8 ounces	227	30	78	822	68%
Tongue, cooked	8 ounces	227	32	20	308	68%
Cold Cuts, Lunch Meat, Sausage						
Bologna	4 ounces	114	15	31	345	68%
Braunschweiger	4 ounces	114	17	31	362	68%
Brown-and-serve sausage, cooked	4 ounces	114	18	48	478	68%
Capicolo	4 ounces	114	23	52	553	68%
Deviled ham	4 ounces	114	7	36	182	68%
Cervelat	4 ounces	114	21	28	351	68%
Frankfurter	4 ounces	114	14	31	344	68%

Ham, boiled, sliced	4 ounces	114	22	20	270	68%
Headcheese	4 ounces	114	17	25	304	68%
Liverwurst	4 ounces	114	18	29	348	68%
Polish sausage, cooked	4 ounces	114	18	29	348	68%
Pork links, cooked	4 ounces	114	20	50	540	68%
Salami, dry	4 ounces	114	28	44	460	68%
Salami, cooked	4 ounces	114	20	28	360	68%
Spam	4 ounces	114	16	29	307	68%
Eggs						
Boiled or poached	2 medium	100	13	11	158	88%
Custard, baked	1 cup	248	13	14	285	88%
Eggnog, all milk	1 cup	310	14	15	192	88%
Omelet	2 medium	100	12	17	201	88%
Scrambled	2 medium	100	12	17	201	88%
White	2 medium	62	7	trace	32	88%
Yolk	2 medium	34	5	10	116	88%
Fish						
Abalone, fried	8 ounces	227	40	1.2	171	78%
Bass, baked	8 ounces	227	43	2.5	195	78%
Bluefish, broiled with butter	8 ounces	227	44	72	177	78%
Clams, fresh, steamed	8 ounces	227	18	2.5	95	78%
Cod, baked	8 ounces	227	38	1	370	78%
Crabmeat, fresh, cooked	8 ounces	227	34	4	200	78%

PROTEIN FROM ANIMAL SOURCES, CONTINUED

FOOD	QUANTITY	WEIGHT (GRAMS)	PROTEIN (GRAMS)	FAT (GRAMS)	CALORIES	PROTEIN ABSORBED & CONVERTED INTO MUSCLE TISSUE
Fish, Continued						
Fishsticks, frozen, breaded, cooked	8 ounces	227	36	20	400	78%
Flounder, baked	8 ounces	227	36	1.5	158	78%
Haddock, fried	8 ounces	227	40	.5	165	78%
Halibut, broiled with butter	8 ounces	227	44	2	194	78%
Herring, kippered	2 small	200	38	10	242	78%
Herring, pickled	8 ounces	227	38	10	242	78%
Lobster, steamed	8 ounces	227	37	3	179	78%
Oysters, raw	1 cup	238	25	5	150	78%
Oysters, cooked	1 cup	238	84	10	174	78%
Perch, yellow broiled	8 ounces	227	44	2	195	78%
Pike, blue broiled	8 ounces	227	41	2	182	78%
Red snapper, grilled	8 ounces	227	45	2	198	78%
Salmon, canned	8 ounces	227	41	13	315	78%
Salmon, fresh, broiled	8 ounces	227	43	14	298	78%
Scallops, steamed	8 ounces	227	35	.5	183	78%
Shrimp, boiled or steamed	8 ounces	227	41	1.5	206	78%
Squid, poached, steamed	8 ounces	227	37	2	190	78%

Sturgeon, poached	8 ounces	227	41	4	210	78%
Swordfish, broiled	8 ounces	227	42	9	249	78%
Trout, grilled	8 ounces	227	46	24	400	78%
Tuna in oil	8 ounces	227	55	46	653	78%
Tuna in water	8 ounces	227	63	1.5	288	78%
Turtle, steamed	8 ounces	227	45	1	202	78%
Game						
Deer, grilled	8 ounces	227	34	60	676	68%
Pheasant, baked	8 ounces	227	52	12	308	68%
Rabbit, stewed	8 ounces	227	46	18	346	68%
Lamb						
Chops, broiled	8 ounces	227	33	65	717	68%
Leg, roasted	8 ounces	227	33	60	672	68%
Shoulder, stewed	8 ounces	227	32	65	713	68%
Pork						
Bacon, fried crisp or broiled	8 ounces	227	10	75	715	68%
Bacon, Canadian, fried	8 ounces	227	21	16	228	68%
Chops, broiled	8 ounces	227	20	125	1205	68%
Ham, smoked, baked	8 ounces	227	35	60	680	68%
Roast	8 ounces	227	20	125	1205	68%
Spareribs, braised	8 ounces	227	28	85	877	68%

PROTEIN FROM ANIMAL SOURCES, CONTINUED

FOOD	QUANTITY	WEIGHT (GRAMS)	PROTEIN (GRAMS)	FAT (GRAMS)	CALORIES	PROTEIN ABSORBED & CONVERTED INTO MUSCLE TISSUE
Poultry						
Chicken, dark meat, broiled	8 ounces	227	40	15	295	68%
Chicken, white meat, broiled	8 ounces	227	40	14	286	68%
Chicken liver, sautéed	8 ounces	227	43	8	254	68%
Duck, roasted	8 ounces	227	36	65	738	68%
Goose, roasted	8 ounces	227	35	75	815	68%
Turkey, dark meat, roasted	8 ounces	227	44	10	266	68%
Turkey, white meat, roasted	8 ounces	227	44	9	257	68%
Veal						
Cutlet, broiled	8 ounces	227	40	43	547	68%
Chops	8 ounces	227	40	45	565	68%
Roast	8 ounces	227	40	43	547	68%

PROTEIN FROM ANIMAL SOURCES: DAIRY PRODUCTS

FOOD	QUANTITY	WEIGHT (GRAMS)	PROTEIN (GRAMS)	FAT (GRAMS)	CARBOHYDRATES (GRAMS)	CALORIES	PROTEIN ABSORBED & CONVERTED INTO MUSCLE TISSUE
Cheese							
American	2 ounces	57	14	16	3	212	76%
Blue	2 ounces	57	12	18	0	210	76%
Cheddar	2 ounces	57	14	18	3	230	76%
Cottage, creamed	1 cup	227	31	9	8	242	76%
Cottage, whole curd	1 cup	227	38	1	8	193	76%
Cream	3 ounce pkg	85	7	32	4	322	76%
Edam	2 ounces	57	13	15	1	195	76%
Feta	2 ounces	57	8	12	1	144	76%
Gouda	2 ounces	57	14	15	1.5	197	76%
Mozzarella (part skim)	2 ounces	57	13	9	1.5	139	76%
Muenster	2 ounces	57	13	17	.5	207	76%
Parmesan, grated	1 tablespoon	5	2	2	0	26	76%
Provolone	2 ounces	57	15	14.5	1	194	76%
Ricotta (whole milk)	2 ounces	57	6.5	7	1	93	76%
Ricotta (part skim)	2 ounces	57	6	4.5	3	77	76%
Roquefort	2 ounces	57	12	17	1	205	76%
Tilsit	2 ounces	57	13	15	1	195	76%
Swiss	2 ounces	57	16	16	0	208	76%
Milk and Cream							
Buttermilk from skim milk	1 cup	244	8	2	10	90	76%
Chocolate milk (1% fat)	1 cup	250	8	2.5	26	167	76%

PROTEIN FROM ANIMAL SOURCES: DAIRY PRODUCTS, CONTINUED

FOOD	QUANTITY	WEIGHT (GRAMS)	PROTEIN (GRAMS)	FAT (GRAMS)	CARBOHYDRATES (GRAMS)	CALORIES	PROTEIN ABSORBED & CONVERTED INTO MUSCLE TISSUE
Milk and Cream, Continued							
Half-and-half	1 cup	240	7	28	10	312	74%
Heavy cream	1 tablespoon	16	.5	5.5	23	52	74%
Milk shake							
chocolate, thick	1 cup	344	11	18	58	421	74%
vanilla, thick	1 cup	344	13	11	61	387	74%
Partly skimmed milk, 2% nonfat milk solids							
added	1 cup	246	8	5	12	125	76%
Skimmed milk	1 cup	245	8	1	12	89	76%
Sour cream	1 tablespoon	12	4	2.5	.5	28	76%
Whole milk	1 cup	244	8	9	11.5	159	76%
Yogurt, no fruit							
made with skimmed milk	1 cup	227	13	.5	18	129	76%
made with whole milk	1 cup	227	8	7.5	11	146	76%
Yogurt, no sugar with fruit,							
whole milk	1 cup	227	9	9	30	250	76%

PROTEIN FROM PLANT SOURCES: BREAD, CEREAL, FLOUR FOODS, FRUIT, NUTS, RICE, SEEDS, VEGETABLES

FOOD	QUANTITY	WEIGHT (GRAMS)	PROTEIN (GRAMS)	FAT (GRAMS)	CARBOHYDRATES (GRAMS)	CALORIES	PROTEIN ABSORBED & CONVERTED INTO MUSCLE TISSUE
Bread							
Bagel, egg or water	1 bagel	55	6	2	31	166	22%
Corn	1 portion	100	7	7	29	207	40%
French or Italian	1 slice	20	2	.4	11	56	15%
Pumpernickel	1 slice	32	3	3	16	80	21%
Rye	1 slice	23	2	.4	11	56	21%
White, enriched	1 slice	23	2	.5	12	61	15%
Whole wheat	1 slice	23	3	.4	10	56	21%
Cereal							
Barley, pearl, uncooked	½ cup	100	8	1	77	349	54%
Bran flakes 40%	1 cup	40	4	.5	27	144	48%
Cornflakes	1 cup	25	2	trace	21	92	40%
Corn grits, cooked	1 cup	243	3	trace	28	124	40%
Cornmeal, cooked	1 cup	240	.3	.5	28	118	40%
Cream of wheat, cooked	1 cup	200	5	.5	27	133	48%
Farina, cooked	1 cup	238	3	trace	22	100	48%
Oatmeal, cooked	1 cup	236	5	2	23	130	48%
Puffed wheat	1 cup	14	1	.5	12	57	48%
Rice polishings	1 cup	100	12	13	25	265	48%
Shredded wheat	1 large	28	4	.5	20	101	48%
Wheat germ	1 tablespoon	6	2	1	2	25	48%

PROTEIN FROM PLANT SOURCES, CONTINUED

FOOD	QUANTITY	WEIGHT (GRAMS)	PROTEIN (GRAMS)	FAT (GRAMS)	CARBOHYDRATES (GRAMS)	CALORIES	PROTEIN ABSORBED & CONVERTED INTO MUSCLE TISSUE
Cereal, Continued							
Wheat germ cereal, cooked	1 cup	65	20	8	25	252	48%
Wheat, bulgur, cooked	1 cup	250	16	2	84	420	48%
Flour Foods							
Macaroni and spaghetti, cooked firm (8-10 minutes)	1 cup	130	6	1	39	189	48%
Noodles, egg, cooked tender (5-6 minutes)	1 cup	160	7	2	38	198	48%
Pancakes							
white flour	1 cake	27	2	2	9	62	15%
buckwheat flour	1 cake	27	2	2	7	54	20%
Pizza, white flour, 14" diameter							
cheese	⅛ portion	75	9	6	24	186	60%
sausage	⅛ portion	100	8	12	23	232	60%
Tortilla, corn, 6" diameter	1 tortilla	30	2	3	7	63	40%
Fruit							
Avocado	1 large	215	5	33	11	361	48%
Banana	1 medium	151	2	trace	29	124	48%
Dates, pitted	1 cup	175	4	1	115	485	48%

Food	Measure						
Grapes							
Concord	1 cup	152	2	1.5	21	105	48%
green seedless	1 cup	200	1	trace	24	100	48%
Grapefruit	1 medium	255	1	trace	44	180	48%
Orange	1 medium	180	2	.5	18	85	48%
Papaya	1 large	400	2	.5	35	152	48%
Pear	1 medium	180	1	1	24	70	48%
Strawberries	1 cup	150	1	.5	12	57	48%
Nuts (shelled)							
Almonds, raw	1 cup	140	26	75	2	785	35%
Brazil, raw	1 cup	300	42	201	2	1985	35%
Cashews, roasted, unsalted	1 cup	100	15	45	26	569	35%
Coconut, fresh	1 cup	100	4	35	4	347	35%
Unsalted Peanuts, roasted	1 cup	240	60	106	51	1398	35%
Peanut butter	1 tablespoon	16	4	8	2	96	35%
Pecans, raw, halves	1 cup	104	10	74	6	730	35%
Pistachios, roasted	1 cup	100	19	53	10	593	35%
Walnuts, raw, halves	1 cup	100	21	60	1	628	35%
Rice (cooked)							
Brown	1 cup	150	4	1	38	177	70%
Instant, white	1 cup	147	3	trace	37	160	60%
White	1 cup	150	3	trace	36	156	63%
Seeds (shelled)							
Pumpkin	1 cup	230	67	106	12	1270	35%
Sesame	1 cup	230	42	122	18	1338	35%
Sunflower	1 cup	100	24	43	19	559	35%

PROTEIN FROM PLANT SOURCES, CONTINUED

FOOD	QUANTITY	WEIGHT (GRAMS)	PROTEIN (GRAMS)	FAT (GRAMS)	CARBOHYDRATES (GRAMS)	CALORIES	PROTEIN ABSORBED & CONVERTED INTO MUSCLE TISSUE
Vegetables							
Beans							
Lima							
fresh, cooked	1 cup	170	13	1	32	189	48%
dry, cooked	1 cup	190	16	1	47	261	48%
Navy, dry, cooked	1 cup	190	15	1	39	225	48%
Red, kidney, dry, cooked	1 cup	256	15	1	40	229	39%
Soybean milk	1 cup	92	9	4	6	96	48%
Soybeans, dry, cooked	1 cup	200	16	1	39	229	48%
Sprouts, cooked	1 cup	100	3	trace	4	28	48%
Broccoli, cooked	1 cup	150	5	4	2	64	48%
Cauliflower, steamed	1 cup	120	3	trace	3	24	48%
Collard greens, steamed	1 cup	200	7	1	7	65	48%
Corn, whole kernel from cooked cob	1 cup	200	4	1	27	133	48%
Endive, raw	1 cup	228	4	trace	8	48	48%
Garbanzos (chickpeas) dry, uncooked	½ cup	100	20	4	61	360	48%
Lentils, dry, cooked	1 cup	200	16	trace	37	212	48%
Mustard greens	1 cup	140	3	.5	4	33	48%
Peas, split, cooked	1 cup	200	16	1	39	229	48%
Spinach, steamed	1 cup	100	3	trace	3	24	48%

FOODS TO AVOID: HIGH IN FAT AND/OR CARBOHYDRATES

FOOD	QUANTITY	WEIGHT (GRAMS)	FAT (GRAMS)	CARBOHYDRATES (GRAMS)	CALORIES
Bread Products					
Biscuits	4 ounces	114	20	52	418
Brown-and-serve rolls	4 ounces	114	7.5	57	339
Muffins	4 ounces	114	11-12	49-56	296-356
Sweet rolls	4 ounces	114	10	56	358
Candy					
Caramels	4 ounces	114	11.5	87	452
Chocolate, milk	4 ounces	114	37	64	590
Chocolate-covered nuts	4 ounces	114	50	45	645
Chocolate-covered raisins	4 ounces	114	19	80	482
Fudge	4 ounces	114	14	86	453
Peanut bars	4 ounces	114	36	54	584
Cake and Pastry					
Carrot	4 ounces	114	21	50	400
Chocolate, with icing	4 ounces	114	19	63	418
Danish, fruit-filled	4 ounces	114	26	50	478
Fruitcake	4 ounces	114	17	68	430
Pound	4 ounces	114	33	53	536
Yellow, with chocolate icing	4 ounces	114	15	68	414

FOODS TO AVOID: HIGH IN FAT AND/OR CARBOHYDRATES

FOOD	QUANTITY	WEIGHT (GRAMS)	FAT (GRAMS)	CARBOHYDRATES (GRAMS)	CALORIES
Cookies					
Brownies with nuts	4 ounces	114	23	80	544
Chocolate chip	4 ounces	114	34	68	585
Fig bars	4 ounces	114	6	85	406
Macaroons	4 ounces	114	26	75	539
Oatmeal, with raisins	4 ounces	114	17	83	512
Sandwich, creme	4 ounces	114	26	79	561
Shortbread	4 ounces	114	26	74	565
Crackers					
Cheese and peanut butter	1 average	7	2	3	35
Graham, chocolate-covered	1 average	13	3	9	61
Matzo	1 piece	20	.3	17	78
Donuts					
Cake	1 average	32	6	17	125
Cream-filled	1 average	35	5	16	122
Raised	1 average	30	8	11	124
Fats and Oils					
Butter	1 teaspoon	5	4	0	36
Margarine	1 teaspoon	5	4	0	36
Oil	1 tablespoon	14	14	0	124

Pie

Banana custard	4 ounces	114	11	35	250
Boston cream	4 ounces	114	11	57	342
Chocolate chiffon	4 ounces	114	17	50	372
Coconut custard	4 ounces	114	14	28	267
Fruit	4 ounces	114	9-13	35-50	225-306
Mince	4 ounces	114	13	47	307
Lemon meringue	4 ounces	114	11	43	289
Pecan	4 ounces	114	26	58	474
Pumpkin	4 ounces	114	13	27	239
Sweet potato	4 ounces	114	13	27	241

Salad Dressings

Blue and roquefort	2 ounces	57	30	4	286
French	2 ounces	57	22	20	232
Italian	2 ounces	57	34	14	313
Mayonnaise	2 ounces	57	90	2	407
Thousand island	2 ounces	57	28	17	284

Salads With Mayonnaise Dressing

Chicken	1 cup	200	15	8	254
Coleslaw	1 cup	120	17	6	120
Egg	1 cup	240	75	4	780

FOODS TO AVOID, CONTINUED

FOOD	QUANTITY	WEIGHT (GRAMS)	FAT (GRAMS)	CARBOHYDRATES (GRAMS)	CALORIES
Macaroni	1 cup	190	12	49	335
Potato	1 cup	250	23	34	362
Tuna	1 cup	200	21	7	340
Snack Foods					
Popcorn, popped plain	4 ounces	114	5.5	86	438
oil and salt added	4 ounces	114	25	70	517
Potato chips	4 ounces	114	45	57	644
Pretzels	4 ounces	114	5	86	442
Sodas					
Colas	1 cup	240	0	24	86
Fruit-flavored	1 cup	240	0	29	110
Ginger ale	1 cup	240	0	19	74
Ice cream	1 cup	345	7	49	262
Root beer	1 cup	240	0	25	98
Seven-up	1 cup	230	0	23	92
Lemon-lime	1 cup	230	0	23	92

LOW-FAT SOURCES OF CARBOHYDRATES

FOOD	QUANTITY	WEIGHT (GRAMS)	CARBOHYDRATES (GRAMS)	PROTEIN (GRAMS)	CALORIES
Bread					
French or Italian	1 slice	20	11	2	56
Rye	1 slice	23	11	2	56
White, enriched	1 slice	23	12	2	61
Whole wheat	1 slice	23	10	3	56
Cereal					
Bran flakes 40%	1 cup	40	27	4	140
Cornflakes	1 cup	25	21	2	92
Corn grits, cooked	1 cup	243	28	3	124
Cornmeal, cooked	1 cup	240	28	.3	118
Cream of wheat, cooked	1 cup	200	27	5	123
Farina, cooked	1 cup	238	22	3	100
Puffed wheat	1 cup	14	12	1	57
Shredded wheat	1 large	28	20	4	101
Fruit (Fresh)					
Apple	1 medium	150	18	trace	110
Apricots	3 medium	114	14	1	55
Banana	1 medium	151	29	2	124
Cantaloupe	½ medium	385	14	1	160
Cherries	1 cup	130	20	2	80
Figs	3 small	114	23	1	90
Grapefruit	½ medium	285	14	1	55

LOW-FAT SOURCES OF CARBOHYDRATES, CONTINUED

FOOD	QUANTITY	WEIGHT (GRAMS)	CARBOHYDRATES (GRAMS)	PROTEIN (GRAMS)	CALORIES
Grapes					
Concord	1 cup	152	21	2	105
green seedless	1 cup	200	24	1	100
muscat or Tokay	1 cup	160	25	1	95
Lemon	1 medium	106	6	1	20
Orange	1 medium	180	18	2	85
Papaya, diced	1 cup	182	18	1	70
Peach	1 medium	114	10	1	35
Pear	1 medium	182	24	1	70
Pineapple, diced	1 cup	140	19	1	75
Plum	1 medium	60	7	trace	25
Strawberries	1 cup	150	12	1	57
Tangerine	1 medium	114	10	1	40
Watermelon	1 wedge	925	27	2	115
Rice (Cooked)					
Brown	1 cup	150	38	4	177
Instant, white	1 cup	147	37	3	166
White	1 cup	150	38	4	177
Vegetables (Fresh)					
Asparagus, cooked	1 cup	175	6	4	135
Beans					
lima, cooked	1 cup	170	32	13	189
snap, green, cooked	1 cup	125	7	2	30

Beets, diced, cooked	1 cup	165	12	2	50
Broccoli, cooked	1 cup	150	2	5	64
Cabbage, cooked	1 cup	170	7	2	35
Carrots, sliced, cooked	1 cup	145	10	1	45
Vegetables (Fresh), Continued					
Cauliflower, flowerets, cooked	1 cup	120	3	3	24
Celery, raw	1 large stalk	40	2	trace	5
Collard greens, cooked	1 cup	200	7	7	65
Corn, whole kernels from cob, cooked	1 cup	200	27	4	133
Cucumber, raw	1 medium	207	7	1	30
Endive, raw	1 cup	228	8	4	48
Lettuce, raw	1 head	220	6	3	30
Mustard greens, cooked	1 cup	140	4	3	33
Onions, raw	1 medium	110	10	2	40
Peas, cooked	1 cup	160	19	9	115
Potato, baked	1 medium	99	21	3	90
Spinach, cooked	1 cup	100	3	3	24
Sprouts, bean, cooked	1 cup	100	4	3	28
Tomato, raw	1 medium	150	7	2	35
Turnip greens, cooked	1 cup	145	5	3	30
Yams, baked	1 medium	110	36	2	155

GLOSSARY

Absorption: The taking in of nutrients from the intestines into the bloodstream.

Adrenal glands: Triangular-shaped organs, located above each kidney, that produce adrenaline.

Alimentary canal: The mucous-membrane-lined tube of the digestive system, extending from the mouth to the anus.

Amino acids: A large group of organic compounds from which proteins are constructed.

Anabolism: The formation of new tissue.

Anemia: A reduction in the number of red blood cells in hemoglobin.

Antioxidants: Substances that protect other substances from changes caused by oxidation.

Assimilate: To transform nutrients into living tissue.

ATP: Abbreviation for *adenosine triphosphate,* the main source of energy for muscular work.

Atrophy: The wasting away of cells, tissues, or organs.

Bacteria: One-celled organisms that may be beneficial, harmful, or useless in the body systems.

Bile: A liquid manufactured by the liver that helps in the digestion of fats.

Blackstrap molasses: A thick syrup made from the final extraction of nutrients from cane or beet sugar.

Body systems: The cardiovascular, central nervous, digestive, endocrine, excretory, muscular, reproductive, and respiratory systems.

Bonemeal: A powdery, flourlike substance made from the bones of cattle.

Brewer's yeast: The dried, pulverized cells of a top-grade yeast used as a source of B-complex vitamins and protein.

Bulgur flour: A cracked wheat that retains the bran and germ of the grain.

Capillary: A tiny blood vessel that connects the arteries and veins.

Carcinoma: Any of several types of cancer.

Cardiovascular: Pertaining to the heart and blood vessels.

Carotene: An orange-yellow pigment found in plants that converts to vitamin A in animal liver.

Catabolism: A metabolic transformation of nutrients or complex substances into simple compounds accompanied by a release of energy.

Catalyst: A substance that changes, especially speeding, the rate of a chemical reaction without being destroyed or altered in the process.

Central nervous system: The brain and spinal cord.

Chelation: A conversion of supplements into an easily digestible form.

Cholesterol: A white, fatlike substance found mostly in the bile, gallstones, brain, blood cells, plasma, egg yolk, and all animal fats.

Chronic: Long and drawn out.

Circulatory system: The method by which blood and lymph are transported throughout the body.

Cirrhosis: A chronic disease of the liver that turns it orange-yellow and ultimately results in liver failure.

Coagulation: Clotting of the blood.

Coenzyme: Most often a vitamin that is essential for enzyme action.

Colitis: Inflammation of the mucous membranes lining the colon.

Colon: The large intestine.

The joy of eating lies in the right company and the right food.

Compound: Anything made up of two or more parts or substances.

Degeneration: A biological change in tissues or organs leading to their loss of vitality and ability to function.

Dehydration: A drying out and shrinking of tissues due to an excessive loss of water from the body.

Desiccated liver: Dried cattle liver sold as a dietary supplement.

Digestive system: The alimentary canal together with accessory glands, including the salivary glands, liver, pancreas, and gallbladder.

Diuretic: A substance that increases the flow of urine from the body.

DNA: Abbreviation for *deoxyribonucleic acid,* a chemical substance in cell nuclei, forming part of the basis for hereditary characteristics.

Dysfunction: An abnormal, impaired, or incomplete functioning of an organ.

Ectomorph: A body type that is slim and linear with long muscles.

Eczema: A skin disease characterized by inflammation, itching, and the formation of scales.

Electrolytes: Substances that become electrically charged in solutions.

Emulsify: To form a fluid consisting of minute oily particles suspended in a liquid.

Endomorph: A body type that is usually overweight due to a slow rate of metabolism.

Enzyme: A protein substance found most often in digestive juices that acts upon food, causing its breakdown into simple compounds.

Estrogen: A female sex hormone.

Fat-soluble vitamin: A vitamin able to dissolve only in fat or oil.

Fatty acids: A large group of organic acids that give fats various melting points, flavors, and textures.

Gastrointestinal: Referring to the intestines and stomach.

Ginkgo seeds: A large seed with a somewhat fishy taste used by the Japanese to promote digestion.

Glucose: A prime source of energy derived from the assimilation of carbohydrates in the body; blood sugar.

Glycogen: A form in which carbohydrates are stored in the body for future conversion into energy needed for muscular work.

Gram: A measurement of weight equaling about 1/28 of an ounce.

Hemoglobin: The oxygen-bearing, iron-containing protein in red blood cells.

Histamine: A substance released by the tissues in allergic reactions.

Hormone: A substance formed chiefly in the endocrine organs and transported to other organs to increase their functional activity.

Hydrochloric acid: A liquid produced by the gastric glands that is essential to proper digestion.

Hypoglycemia: A condition caused by abnormally low blood sugar.

Inorganic: Substances not of plant or animal origin.

Insulin: A hormone secreted by the pancreas, essential to regulating the metabolism of sugar.

Intestinal flora: Bacteria found in the intestines that are necessary for digestion and metabolism of many nutrients.

Lecithin: A waxy substance found in eggs, blood, bile, brain, nerves, and other animal tissues.

Linoleic acid: One of the unsaturated fats essential to life; a constituent of vitamin F.

Lipid: Any organic compounds consisting of fats or fatlike substances insoluble in water.

Lipoproteins: Proteins combined with fatty substances.

Lymph: A clear yellowish fluid resembling blood plasma and found in the lymph vessels and tissue spaces.

Mcg: Abbreviation for *microgram;* 1/1,000 of a milligram.

Mesomorph: A body type that is naturally muscular with a good skeletal structure.

Metabolism: A chemical process by which nutrients from food are converted into energy and protoplasm is produced to build and repair body tissue.

Mg: Abbreviation for *milligram;* 1/1,000 of a gram.

Mitosis: The process of cell reproduction.

Nervous system: The network of brain, spinal cord, and nerve cells that coordinates and regulates all body activity.

Nutrient: Any substance that supplies the body with elements vital to life support.

Ovolactovegetarians: Individuals on diets excluding all food from animal sources except milk products and eggs.

Oxidation: The union of a substance with oxygen.

Parathyroid glands: A set of small organs alongside the thyroid that secretes hormones, increasing the calcium content of the blood.

Peptidases: Enzymes that convert peptides into amino acids.

Phytic acid: A substance containing calcium or magnesium salts; found most often in cereal.

Pituitary gland: A small organ located at the base of the brain that secretes hormones essential to life support and growth.

Pure vegetarian: An individual on a diet that excludes all foods of animal origin.

Pyruvic acid: An organic acid involved in the metabolism of proteins, fats, and carbohydrates.

Rice polishings: The inner bran layers of rice that are rubbed off in milling.

RNA: Abbreviation for *ribonucleic acid,* a carrier of genetic information to the cells.

Rose hips: Nodules underneath rosebuds that are a rich source of vitamin C.

Supplement: Any substance in the form of a pill, powder, or liquid that supplies nutrients.

Sulfonamides: Medications containing sulfa drugs.

Synthesis: The formation of complex compounds into simple substances.

Thyroid gland: A small organ located at the base of the neck that secretes hormones regulating body growth.

Torula yeast: A bitter-tasting nutritional supplement that is a rich source of the B-complex vitamins.

Toxicity: The quality of being harmful, destructive, or poisonous.

Trace elements: Any substance necessary in the human diet in minute amounts of less than 100 mcg daily.

Water-soluble vitamin: Vitamins that dissolve in water.

Wheat germ: The heart of the wheat kernel.

Zen macrobiotic diet: A dietary program high in brown rice almost to the exclusion of other carbohydrates and proteins and fats. Not recommended in this book.

INDEX

161